How to Train Your
Poodle

liz palika

Photo by Isabelle Francais

POODLES

Photos by the author unless
otherwise credited.

The publisher would like to thank all of the owners of dogs pictured in this book, including the following: Robin Ashback, Judy Barkai, DeWitt Bolden, Gayle Bryan, Joan G. Brenneke, Deborah Butler, Glenna Carlson, Ann Curwen, Bob and Judy Dumond, Sheryl Emerson, Linda Gambino, Neil Goren, Maryann K. Howarth, James Johnson, Cheryl Ann Martin, Cherie Metz, Sandra Pearce, Eileen S. Price, Jan Price, Frances E. Shrader, Martin Simon, Patricia A. Zbock

© T.F.H. Publications, Inc.

Distributed in the UNITED STATES to the Pet Trade by T.F.H. Publications, Inc., 1 TFH Plaza, Neptune City, NJ 07753; on the Internet at www.tfh.com; in CANADA by Rolf C. Hagen Inc., 3225 Sartelon St., Montreal, Quebec H4R 1E8; Pet Trade by H & L Pet Supplies Inc., 27 Kingston Crescent, Kitchener, Ontario N2B 2T6; in ENGLAND by T.F.H. Publications, PO Box 74, Havant PO9 5TT; in AUSTRALIA AND THE SOUTH PACIFIC by T.F.H. (Australia), Pty. Ltd., Box 149, Brookvale 2100 N.S.W., Australia; in NEW ZEALAND by Brooklands Aquarium Ltd., 5 McGiven Drive, New Plymouth, RD1 New Zealand; in SOUTH AFRICA by Rolf C. Hagen S.A. (PTY.) LTD., P.O. Box 201199, Durban North 4016, South Africa; in JAPAN by T.F.H. Publications, Japan—Jiro Tsuda, 10-12-3 Ohjidai, Sakura, Chiba 285, Japan. Published by T.F.H. Publications, Inc.
MANUFACTURED IN THE
UNITED STATES OF AMERICA
BY T.F.H. PUBLICATIONS, INC.

Contents

Introduction 4

1 Selecting the Right Dog for You 6

2 Canine Development Stages 20

3 Early Puppy Training 32

4 The Basic Obedience Commands 44

5 All About Formal Training 59

6 Problem Prevention and Solving 68

7 Advanced Training and Dog Sports 80

8 Have Some Fun With Your Training 91

Suggested Reading 96

INTRODUCTION

When I was a child growing up, my mother had Poodles as pets. I was always sneaking the dogs outside with me. We would roam the nearby fields and woods, investigate small animal holes, chase rabbits, and enjoy the beauty of life. As a preteen, my favorite game was tramping through the woods, pretending that I was a pioneer or a settler crossing the Great Plains, with the Poodles as my faithful companions.

I even taught "Sherrill," one of the Poodles, how to ride in a child's passenger bicycle seat. Sherrill would sit in the seat, her eyes half closed and her ears blowing in the wind as I pedaled madly. I knew she loved those rides because whenever I would wheel my bike out of the garage, she would bounce up and down and bark at me until I picked her up.

Although the Poodles had fun playing with me outside, inside the house they had eyes only for my mother. They would snuggle up next to her on the sofa and bark at us if we tried to give Mom a hug. As a teenager, I didn't understand and was often angry at the dogs for what I considered a betrayal. Looking back, I think of their behavior as a mark of their intelligence. Mom was in charge of the house and the dogs were aligning themselves with her power. Smart dogs!

Poodles are more intelligent than most people give them credit for. Unfortunately, people who aren't familiar with the breed see Poodles as show dogs with bizarre haircuts or as the family pet that goes to the groomer's for a fluffy 'do every six weeks. Assuming that a Poodle is all fluff and no substance is invalid and untrue.

Poodle owners will readily tell you that their dogs are in a class of their own. In fact, as my mother often said, "Suzette and Sherrill were not dogs, they were Poodles, thank you very much!"

As many children and former children can attest, Poodles are faithful companions for kids of all ages.

It's simply not correct that Poodles are all fluff and no substance. They are smart, athletic dogs with big hearts and friendly grins.

p o o d l e s

SELECTING
the Right Dog for You

WHAT ARE POODLES?

Although there are several theories, it is not known where Poodles originally developed. Like many other breeds, historical accounts are either nonexistent or very sketchy. However, the Poodle has been noted in literary references and depicted in artwork by such artists as Albrecht Durer that dates back to the 15th and 16th centuries. These paintings give us a clear picture of the Poodle's development in parts of Europe.

FAMOUS ARTWORK

A very famous 18th century painting by Thomas Gainsborough depicts his daughters and a dog that looks very much like an ungroomed version of the white Poodle that we know today. Jean-Baptiste Oudry painted "Fancy" in the 18th century, which shows a clipped dog with a curly topknot and a puff on the end of the tail—very Poodle-like. John Chalon painted a woman trimming a very curly-coated dog while the other

The noble Poodle appears in Europe's great literature and artwork throughout several centuries.

Photo by Isabelle Francais

dogs at her feet showed off their coats. Other 18th century artists, including Goya, featured Poodles or the Poodle's ancestors. Several historical accounts agree that the breed's ancestors were probably a German gun dog, called the Pudel, and a French retrieving breed, called the Barbet. In fact, the name Poodle probably came from the German breed, Pudel. Relatives of the Poodle most likely include the Irish, Portuguese, and Spanish Water Spaniels, and the Hungarian Puli.

NATIONAL DOG OF FRANCE

The American Kennel Club's (AKC) *The Complete Dog Book* states that the Poodle "has been regarded as the national dog of France, where it is known as the Caniche, derived from chien canard, or duck dog."

Although the Poodle's ancestry may be debatable, it is a fact that the Poodle was a hard-working water retriever. An excellent swimmer, the Poodle successfully retrieved birds, especially ducks and geese, from water. He was able to tolerate very cold water because the untrimmed, thick, curly coat served as good insulation. With his probable

> **CHURCHILL AND RUFUS**
> Winston Churchill was a Poodle owner. His Poodles, Rufus and Rufus II, were often seen riding on Churchill's lap when out in public.

relation to the Hungarian Puli, the Poodle has also been used as a herding or livestock dog.

In the 18th and 19th centuries, the Poodle was a favorite circus performer due to his agility, athleticism, and trainability. Circus Poodles were taught to walk on their back legs, dance, play cards or dominos, wear costumes, ride small bicycles and horses, and do any number of other complicated or daring tricks.

Circus Poodles of the 18th and 19th centuries were frequently trained to walk and dance on their hind legs.

Photo by Robert Smith

POODLES TODAY

Today's Poodle is still a hard-working dog when given the chance. Intelligent and adaptable, Poodles have excellent eyesight, a sharp sense of smell, and very good hearing. These attributes have led people to use Poodles in a variety of occupations, including trackers, search and rescue dogs, retrievers, service dogs, and therapy dogs.

The Poodle should always appear elegant, standing tall and carrying himself proudly. Their regal bearing causes many people to think that Poodles are taller and larger than they actually are.

Standard Poodles are taller than 15 inches at the shoulder. Miniature Poodles are taller

Poodles come in many colors and sizes. Here, two Standard Poodles pose with a Miniature Poodle.

Photo by Isabelle Francais

than 10 inches at the shoulder, but less than 15 inches. Toy Poodles are less than 10 inches tall at the shoulder.

The Poodle's head is long, with a long, straight, fine muzzle. The eyes are dark, oval, and positioned to emphasize an alert, intelligent expression. The ears hang close to the head, at or below the level of the eyes, and are heavily coated.

The Poodle's body and leg length should create a square. The length of the body from breastbone to the point of the rump should equal the dog's height from the point of the shoulder to the ground. The body is not overly muscled or heavy, but athletic and lean.

The Poodle's coat is one of his defining features, ranging in color from white, cream, apricot, or café-au-lait to cocoa brown, black, or silver. Although spotted or parti-colored dogs are sometimes seen, they are not allowed to compete in conformation dog shows and are not considered a desirable color. The Poodle's coat is naturally curly, coarse in texture, and should be dense and thick.

TEMPERAMENT

The Poodle is alert, active, intelligent, proud, and always

Photo by Isabelle Francais

Poodles bond closely with their owners and need to spend a great deal of time with their families.

carries himself with an air of dignity. Poodles are very affectionate animals that bond easily with their people. They need to spend a lot of time with their owners playing, learning social rules, and cuddling.

Benjamin L. Hart and Lynette A. Hart, authors of *The Perfect Puppy*, said of the Standard Poodle, "If you select a Standard Poodle, you will be selecting one of the top-ranked breeds in trainability." They continued by saying that the Standard Poodle is easy to obedience train as well as housetrain. This size Poodle is very playful, usually good with

Standard and Miniature Poodles make the best pets for families with kids. These two babies—a Mini and his little boy—will be buddies for life.

Photo by Isabelle Francais

children, and yet is not overly excitable.

The Miniature Poodle is the most popular size Poodle and the most affectionate. He is also easily trained, both in obedience and housetraining. The Miniature Poodle is more active than the larger size, and more reactive, meaning that he is quicker to react to things around him than the Standard Poodle. It also suggests that there may be more activity and barking.

The Toy Poodle is also an affectionate and easily trainable dog, but not as much as the Miniature or the Standard. They seem to be more reactive as well. The Harts said, "The Toy Poodle would appear to be not as good a choice for a family pet as the Miniature or Standard because of his higher rankings on snapping at children."

Bruce Fogle, DVM, a noted canine behaviorist, warns that Toy Poodles may not be the easiest breed to housetrain, ranking them far below the other two Poodle sizes and below the all-breed average. (*Behavior Profile Behavior Charts; Dog Breed Handbooks.*)

Poodles can be protective and will bark at strangers, which is a trait often desired by dog owners. However, shyness and fearfulness are sometimes seen in Poodles, especially with the smaller sizes, but these are not desirable personality traits.

Do not leave your Poodle home alone for long periods of time. Left alone for too long, Poodles may become morose, destructive, and possibly problem barkers. Poodles need training; not only to learn household and social rules, but also to keep their intelligent mind sharp. A bored Poodle is going to get into trouble.

A Poodle of any age or size will fit the lifestyle of a retired person with plenty of time to devote to a dog.

IS A POODLE THE RIGHT DOG FOR YOU? Evaluating Your Personality and Lifestyle

The decision to add a dog to your family is not something to be taken lightly. Standard and Miniature Poodles often live 12 to 14 years, with Toy Poodles routinely living even longer.

Do you work long hours and often come home tired? Would you rather relax than take care of a puppy when you get home? Then perhaps an older Toy Poodle would be a good choice for you. A puppy would require more time than you have, and Miniature Poodles are much more active than Toys. However, even an adult Toy Poodle is going to need your time and energy. If you can't provide those things, then you might want to rethink your decision to get a dog.

Do you work long hours but enjoy doing things outside, such as riding a bicycle? If so, a Standard Poodle might suit your lifestyle. Standards, although less active than Miniatures, would love to run alongside your bike for exercise. However, an adult still might be a better choice than a puppy.

Do you work at home and keep relatively short hours? Are you retired and have a lot of time for a dog? If so, take your pick, because any size Poodle might suit your needs. Keep in mind that the smaller the

Poodle, the more reactive and active he will be. In addition, puppies require a lot of time and effort on your part, so think carefully about how much of your time you can devote to a puppy.

You need to understand that Poodles love to be with their owners. If you don't like being touched or followed, then don't get a Poodle, because he will follow you from room to room. When you sit down, your Poodle will be right there with you. When you leave the house, your Poodle will want to go with you. Obviously, having a dog with you 24 hours a day is impossible, but a Poodle will want to spend as much time as he can with you.

The Poodle's Needs

All dogs have specific needs that you should be aware of before you add one to your family. It could mean the difference between having a successful relationship with your dog or giving him up later.

First of all, your companionship and devotion are very important to a Poodle. You must also be willing to take the time to train your Poodle properly. They are very intelligent dogs, and if you don't train your Poodle, he will train you.

Grooming is also an important requirement. A Poodle's coat requires a great deal of upkeep, including daily brushing and combing. If you

Standard Poodles must get regular outdoor exercise in order to be happy and healthy. Potential owners should take that into consideration.

Photo by Isabelle Francais

are willing, you can also learn how to clip your Poodle's coat to keep it at a maintainable length. If not, you will need to pay a groomer to trim the coat, usually about every four to six weeks. Standard Poodles need to exercise on a regular basis. Running alongside a bicycle, jogging with you, or chasing a tennis ball are all excellent activities for your Poodle. Miniature and Toy Poodles can get their exercise in the house, perhaps chasing a ball up and down the hallway.

SELECTING THE RIGHT DOG
Male or Female?

There are many myths concerning the personality traits of both males and females. Ultimately, it depends upon the personality of the individual dog. Spayed bitches (females) and neutered males (dogs) are usually a little calmer than dogs that are not, because removing the sexual hormones eliminates any sexual tension. Your Poodle doesn't necessarily need those hormones to be a good pet and companion.

In most breeds of dog, males are usually larger, taller, and heavier. Although male Standard Poodles are generally taller than females, the

difference can be slight. There are so many size variations in Standard, Miniature, and Toy Poodles that sexual differences are almost nonexistent. You might be able to find very small male Toy Poodles and larger female Miniature Poodles because there is a wide variation.

What Age?

Although Poodle puppies are adorable little fluff balls that are hard to resist, they are a lot of work. In fact, adding a puppy to your family is like having a baby around the house. They eat, sleep, go outside to relieve themselves, play, and then start the cycle all over again. All of these things require your help

How old is your ideal dog? Poodle puppies are cute but time-consuming, and there are many lovely adult dogs waiting for loving homes.

Photo by Isabelle Francais

A rescue group or an animal shelter is a great place to find an adult Poodle to adopt. These animals will be prescreened for temperament and medical problems.

and cooperation. As your Poodle puppy grows, he will become not only an important part of the family, but your best friend.

Adding a Poodle to your family doesn't mean that you must get a puppy. There are many older Poodles that need homes, possibly due to a family member passing away or because their owner was transferred overseas. These dogs may be perfect for someone who wants a Poodle, but doesn't have the time, energy, or patience that it takes to raise a puppy.

Unfortunately, there are some negative factors involved in adopting an adult dog. The adoption process can be compared to buying a used car—sometimes you get a gem and sometimes you get a lemon. When you adopt an older dog, you may not be aware of his habits (good or bad) or any possible behavior problems. How the dog was treated by his previous owner(s) can affect his future behavior. In addition, you may not have any knowledge of the dog's health and previous health care routine.

Newly adopted dogs must also be given the time to adjust to their new home because they may be insecure, fearful, or shy. These dogs usually calm down after they settle in and begin to show their normal Poodle personality within a few months.

Finding an Adult Dog

If you think an adult dog is a better choice for you, there are a few places where you can look for your new companion. Start with the local humane society or nearby shelter because they may have Poodles of different sizes. The shelter will also know if there is a local Poodle rescue group.

Evaluating an Adult Dog

Once you have found an adult dog, how do you decide if

this is the right dog for you? First, ask yourself if you like this particular dog. Your feelings for the dog are a big part of whether or not the relationship will work.

Do you know why the dog was given up by his previous

When evaluating an adult dog, look for one that is happy to see you and unafraid. Make sure you are prepared to deal with any preexisting behavior problems before you decide to adopt the dog.

Photo by Isabelle Francais

owner(s)? If behavior problems were the reason, make sure that you are willing to deal with them until the dog can be trained. Is the dog housetrained? Housetraining an untrained adult dog can be a big undertaking.

How does the dog greet you? What is his personality like? When you talk to him, does he bounce up to you, happy and excited to see you? If you whistle, does he cock his head to the side to listen? Ideally, you want a dog that is curious, happy, and unafraid. If the dog is hiding behind someone, won't look at you, or is trying to hide under or behind the furniture, beware. This is a very fearful, shy, and possible problem dog. However, avoid the dog that stands his ground, up on his tiptoes, staring you in the eye. This is a potentially aggressive dog.

Look for a happy dog that doesn't bark too much and is housetrained. Make sure that you can easily handle the dog and touch his ears, tail, and feet, because Poodles require constant brushing and grooming. Be positive that the dog's behavior problems are minimal enough that you can deal with them for the time being.

Finding a Puppy

If you have the time, patience, and resources that it takes to raise a puppy, you will want to find a reputable breeder. Breeder referrals can come from many sources. Does a neighbor own a nice, well-behaved Poodle? If so, ask her where she acquired him. Your local veterinarian may also know which local breeders consistently produce healthy puppies. Many of the national dog magazines carry advertisements from larger breeders. You also may want to attend a dog show in your area and talk to people who are knowledgeable about the breed.

Once you find a few breeders, make an appointment to meet with them. Be sure to ask them questions.

"Are you active in dog shows and sports?" If breeders actively show their dogs, they are most likely good physical examples of the breed. If they participate in obedience trials, their dogs are trainable.

"Do you belong to the national or regional Poodle clubs?" If the breeder belongs to any Poodle clubs, she is more likely to be up-to-date on news concerning the breed. Breed club newsletters and magazines usually publish articles focusing on the breed's health and well-being.

"What health problems have you seen in your dogs?" If the breeder says none, be skeptical. Poodles are susceptible to a variety of health problems, such as allergies, eye defects, hip dysplasia, and bloat. The breeder should be honest with you regarding potential problems. In addition, she should discuss with you her efforts to ensure that her puppies are not affected.

"Can you provide me with a list of references?" She will provide you with a list of people that she knows will be helpful to you. Ask these people if the breeder followed through with her promises. Did she give them all of the required paperwork, including the puppy's registration? Most important, would they do business with this breeder again?

Caring breeders will also ask you as many questions as you ask them. A conscientious breeder wants to know if you are the right person (or family) for her puppies. Don't be offended by her questions and answer them honestly. If, by some chance, the breeder says that her dogs are not right for you, don't take offense. She knows her dogs better than you do and is trying to ensure that

It's easy to get swept away by a litter of adorable Poodle puppies, but don't forget to ask the breeder some important questions before you buy one of her dogs.

Photo by Isabelle Francais

Photo by Isabelle Francais

Every puppy is different. Select one with a personality that matches yours.

her dogs stay in their new homes for the rest of their lives.

Evaluating a Puppy

Each puppy has his own personality, and finding the right personality to match yours can be a challenge. For example, if you are quiet and retrospective, an outgoing, extroverted, high-energy puppy will drive you to distraction. However, that same puppy would probably make a great pet for someone with an energetic personality.

When you go to look at a litter of puppies, there are a few things that you can do to help evaluate a puppy's personality. Take one of the puppies away from his littermates and mother and go into another room. Place him on the floor and walk a few steps away. Squat down and call the puppy to you. An outgoing, extroverted puppy will come to you right away and try to climb into your lap. If you stand up and walk away, he will follow you, often getting under foot. If you throw a crumpled piece of paper, he will dash after it, shake it a few times, and possibly even bring it back to you. This type of personality will do well with an extroverted, energetic owner.

He will need training to challenge his mind and exercise to work his body.

A quiet, more submissive puppy will come to you when you call, but may do a belly crawl to your feet or roll over and bare his belly. When you get up to walk away, this puppy may watch you but be hesitant to follow. If you toss the paper, he may watch it without going after it, or he may go after it but not bring it back. This puppy will need a quiet owner, gentle handling, and positive training.

These two examples are extremes in Poodle temperament. The vast majority of Poodles fall in between these extremes. Try to find a Poodle with a personality that will be comfortable for you. Don't get a Poodle with a certain personality type and hope to change him because that never works. Find a puppy that is right for you.

BE CAREFUL!

Adding a dog to your family should be a time of joy. Take the time to research your needs thoroughly to ensure that you choose a Poodle that is perfect for you. This dog will be with you for the rest of his life, so make the best choice!

Canine
DEVELOPMENT
Stages

IN THE BEGINNING

Why do we keep dogs as pets? Although dogs perform certain tasks for us, so do many other domestic animals. What makes dog ownership so special? Most dog owners say that the relationship that they have with their dog, the feeling of companionship and devotion, is what makes having a dog so wonderful. When a dog loves you, he doesn't care who you are, what you look like, what your social standing is, or how much money you make. He loves you unconditionally.

The bond or relationship between a dog and his owner may be what makes owning a dog worthwhile, but it doesn't happen automatically. Although puppies may be genetically programmed to bond with people, they must spend time with a new owner to do so. To understand when and how this bond develops, it's important to realize that your Poodle is a dog and not a person in a fuzzy dog suit.

Families and Packs

Most researchers agree that the ancestors to today's dogs

Although Poodles look almost nothing like their ancestors the wolves, they still possess the natural pack mentality. To a modern Poodle, his human family functions as his pack.

Photo by Isabelle Francais

Photo by Isabelle Francais

The special bond between a Poodle and his owner is undeniable, but it doesn't happen automatically. Each puppy must spend time with humans in order to learn how to bond.

were wolves; however, there is some disagreement on what type of wolf. In any event, wolves are social creatures that live in an extended family pack, which consists of a dominant (alpha) male and a dominant (alpha) female that breed. There will also be subordinate males, females, juveniles, and puppies. This is a very harmonious group that hunts together, plays together, defends its territory against intruders, and cares for each other. The only discord occurs when there is a change in the pack order. If one of the leaders becomes disabled, an adult leaves the pack, or a subordinate adult tries to assume dominance, there may be some jockeying around to fill that position.

Many experts feel that domesticated dogs adapt so well to our lifestyle because we also live in groups. We call our groups families instead of packs, but they are still social groups. However, the comparison isn't accurate because our families are much more chaotic than the average wolf pack. We are terribly inconsistent with our social and behavior rules. For example, we let our Poodle jump up and paw us when we're in grubby clothes and yell at him when he jumps up on our good clothes. To a dog, our communication skills are confusing because our voice says one thing while our body language says something else. We can say that both dogs and humans live in social groups and use that comparison to understand a little more about our dogs. However, we must also understand that our families are very different from a wolf pack.

FROM BIRTH TO FOUR WEEKS OF AGE

For the first three weeks of a baby Poodle's life, the family and the pack are unimportant. The only one of any significance is a Poodle's mother, because she is the key to his survival and

For the first few weeks of a Poodle puppy's life, only his mother is important.

Photo by Isabelle Francais

the source of his food, warmth, and security.

At four weeks of age, the baby Poodle's needs are still being met by his mother, but his littermates are becoming more important. His brothers and sisters provide warmth and security when the mother leaves the nest. His curiosity is developing and he will climb on and over his littermates, learning their scent and feel. During this period, he will learn to use his sense of hearing to follow sounds and his sense of vision to follow moving objects.

Also at this time, the baby Poodle's mother begins the discipline process. Starting this process early is extremely important to the puppy's future acceptance of discipline and training.

The breeder should be handling the puppies now to get them used to other people. At this age, the puppies can learn the difference between their mother's touch and gentle handling from people.

WEEKS FIVE THROUGH SEVEN

The young Poodle goes through tremendous changes between five and seven weeks of age. He is learning how to recognize people and is starting to respond to individual voices. He is playing more with his littermates and learning how to get along with the other puppies, how to play correctly, when the play is too rough, when to be submissive, and

As a Poodle puppy grows and develops, his littermates will provide plenty of mental stimulation while mom works hard to keep the puppies in line.

Photo by Robert Pearcy

what to take seriously. His mother's discipline at this stage of development teaches the puppy to accept corrections, training, and affection.

THE EIGHTH WEEK

The eighth week of life is a frightening time for most puppies. They go through several periods of fear during their growing stage, and this is the first one. Even though the eighth week is the average time that most puppies go to their new homes, they would actually benefit by staying with their littermates for one more week. If the puppy leaves the breeder's home during this fear period and is frightened by the car ride home, he may retain that fear for the rest of his life. In fact, this stress is why so many puppies get carsick. The same applies to the puppy's new home, his first trip to the veterinarian's office, or anything else that frightens him.

WEEKS NINE THROUGH TWELVE

The baby Poodle can go to his new home anytime during the ninth and tenth weeks of life. At this age, he is ready to form permanent relationships. Take advantage of this and spend time with your new

LET THE MOTHER DOG CORRECT

Some inexperienced breeders will stop the mother dog from correcting her puppies, perhaps thinking that she is impatient, tired, or a poor mother. When the mother dog is not allowed to correct her puppies naturally, they do not learn how to accept discipline and have a hard time later when their new owner tries to establish some rules. Orphaned puppies raised by people suffer from similar problems. The mother dog instinctively knows what to do for her babies and sometimes a correction—a low growl, a bark, or a snap of the teeth—is exactly what is needed.

The puppies should never be taken from their mother at this stage of development. Those that are sent to new homes too early may have lasting behavior problems. They often have difficulty dealing with other dogs, trouble accepting rules and discipline, and may become excessively shy, aggressive, or fearful.

puppy, playing with him and encouraging him to explore his new world. Teach him his name by calling to him in a happy, high-pitched tone of voice. Encourage him to follow you by backing away from him, patting your leg, and using your voice.

Puppies should be gently handled by humans almost from birth so that they will make good pets when they are old enough to go to new homes.

Photo by Isabelle Francais

During this time, you should begin socializing your new puppy, which is more than simply introducing your puppy to other people, dogs, noises, and sounds. It is making sure that these things do not frighten your baby Poodle as you introduce them. For example, once your baby Poodle has had some vaccinations (check with your veterinarian), take him with you to the pet store when you go to buy dog food. While there, introduce your puppy to the store clerks, other customers, and even to the store parrot. Your trip there could also include walking up some stairs, walking on slippery floors, and going through an automatic door. All of these things, introduced gradually with encouragement and repeated, help make your puppy confident and well-socialized.

During this stage of development, your Poodle puppy's pack instincts are developing. He is beginning to understand who belongs to his pack (or family) and who doesn't. Do not let him growl at visitors during this stage, because he is much too young to understand when and how to protect. Instead, stop the growling and let him know that you, as his pack leader, can protect the family.

You can show your puppy his position in the family several different ways, but one of the easiest is to lay him down, roll him over, and give him a tummy rub. This exercise may seem very simple, but by baring his

Gently and lovingly show your Poodle puppy that you are the boss by having him lie on his back in your arms or on the ground.

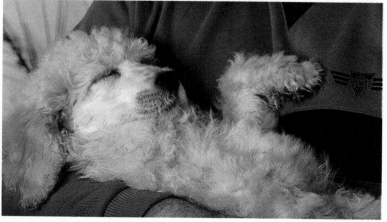

Photo by Isabelle Francais

poodles

tummy, he is assuming a submissive position to you. When his mother corrected him by growling or barking at him, he would roll over and bare his tummy to her, in essence telling her, "Okay! I understand, you're the boss!" When you have him roll over for a tummy rub, you are helping him receive the same message, but you are doing it in a very gentle, loving way.

During this stage of development, discipline is very important. Love, affection, and security are still vital, but right now, your Poodle puppy needs to learn that his life is governed by rules. Don't allow him to do anything now that you won't want him to continue doing later as a full-grown dog.

Photo by Isabelle Francais

Your Poodle must learn from a young age that his life is governed by household rules. The "no dogs on chairs" rule hasn't quite sunk in for these two puppies.

WEEKS THIRTEEN THROUGH SIXTEEN

From 13 through 16 weeks of age, your puppy will be trying to establish his position in your family pack. If you were able to set rules in the earlier stages of development, this won't be difficult.

Consistency in enforcing household rules is very important, and everyone in the family or household should be enforcing the rules in the same way. Poodles are very perceptive and if your puppy senses a weak link in the chain of command, he will take advantage of it. This doesn't mean that he's a bad puppy—it simply means that he's intelligent.

Puppies with dominant personalities may start mounting behavior to small children in the family or to their toys. Obviously, this is undesirable behavior and should be stopped immediately.

WEEKS SEVENTEEN THROUGH TWENTY-SIX

Sometime between 17 and 26 weeks of age, most puppies go

Photo by Isabelle Francais

To teach your Poodle to retrieve, get his attention with a toy he likes and then toss it a few feet away.

through another fear period, much like the one they went through at 8 weeks of age. Things that the puppy accepted as normal may suddenly become frightening.

Make sure that you don't reinforce any of these fears by petting and cuddling him and telling him that it's acceptable to be afraid. He will hear the soft words, feel the petting, and assume that these are positive reinforcements for his fears. Instead, touch the object that is scaring him and say, "Look at this!" in a happy tone of voice so he can see that there is nothing to be afraid of.

Your Poodle's protective

RETRIEVING

Begin retrieving games at 9 to 12 weeks of age. Get your Poodle's attention with a toy he likes and then toss it four to six feet away. When he grabs the toy, call him back to you in a happy tone of voice. Praise him enthusiastically when he brings it back to you. If he runs away and tries to get you to chase him, stand up and walk away, stopping the game completely. Don't chase him! Make him learn early on that he must play the games by your rules. Chasing a ball or a soft flying disc can be great exercise for the puppy. Teaching him to play by your rules also sets the stage for a sound working relationship later.

instincts will continue to develop through this stage. If he continues to show protectiveness or aggression (with growling, snarling, barking, or raised hackles), interrupt his behavior by turning him away or distracting him. If you encourage the behavior or correct it harshly, you will be placing too much emphasis on it and your puppy may continue the incorrect behavior. Overemphasis at this young age may result in an overprotective or fearful dog. Instead, react calmly and stop the bad behavior from happening in the first place.

STOP THE YAPPING!

Many small Poodles may begin barking at this age. Although it may develop for a specific reason, barking can easily turn into a problem. Stop it now before it turns into a chronic problem. Use a firm tone of voice, "Sweetie, quiet!" as you use your hand to gently close the puppy's mouth. As soon as he is quiet, praise him, "Good boy to be quiet!"

THE TEENAGE MONTHS

The teenage experience for a dog is very similar to a human's experience. Humans in their teens strive to prove their

When your puppy passes through a fear stage, things that once seemed normal will suddenly be scary to him. These fears will quickly pass if you do not reinforce them by comforting the puppy.

Photo by Isabelle Francais

ability to take care of themselves. They want to be independent, yet they still want the security of home. These two conflicting needs seem to drive some teens (and their parents) crazy.

Dogs can be very similar. Adolescent Poodles push the boundaries of their rules, trying to see if their owner will be firm. Most Poodle owners say that their dogs in this stage act entirely too full of themselves.

The teenage stage in Poodles usually hits at about 12 months of age, although it's not unusual to see it happen a month or two earlier. You'll know when it happens. One day you will ask your previously well-trained dog to do something he knows very well, such as sit, and he'll look at you as if he's never heard that word before in his life.

Other common behaviors include regressing in social skills. Your previously well-socialized Poodle may start barking at other dogs, jumping on people, getting rough with children, or chasing the cat.

During this stage of development, you will need to consistently enforce social and household rules. Hopefully, you will have already started obedience training because that

Photo by Isabelle Francais

Teenage dogs, like teenage children, can be unruly. They may test their owners, trying to see if the owner will firmly adhere to household rules.

control will help. If you haven't started obedience training at this point, do so now.

Also, make sure that your dog knows you are the leader. This is not the time to be best friends, because that would cause a dominant personality to regard you as weak. Instead, act like the leader. Stand tall when you communicate with your dog and bend over him (not down to him) when you pet him. You should always go first and make him wait and follow you. Also, you should eat before you feed him.

As the leader, you can give your dog permission to do things. For example, if he goes to pick up a toy for you to throw, give him permission to do it, "Good boy to bring me your toy!" If he lies down at your feet (by his own choice) tell him, "Good boy to lie down!" By giving him permission and praising him, you are putting yourself in control.

You need to understand that this rebellion is not aimed at you. It is a very natural part of growing up and it will pass. Your Poodle will eventually grow up, because the adolescent stage usually only lasts a few months.

GROWING UP

Standard Poodles are not usually mentally or physically mature until they are three years old. Toy and Miniature Poodles mature more quickly at two years of age. Usually, bitches (females) mature a little earlier than the males.

After the teenage stage but before maturity, your Poodle may go through another fear period. This usually hits at about 14 months of age, but may be later. Handle this period like you did the others, and don't reinforce your dog's fears. Fortunately, this is usually the last fear period that your dog will experience.

At about two years of age, your Poodle may go through another challenging period to find out if you really are the boss. Treat this period as you did the teenage stage. Enforce the rules and praise your puppy for good behavior.

When your Poodle reaches his third birthday, throw a party! By this time, he is usually considered full grown. However, adulthood to a Poodle doesn't always mean that life is serious. Poodles definitely like to have fun!

When your Poodle reaches his third birthday and is "officially" grown up, why not throw him a party? Costumes, of course, are optional.

Early
PUPPY
Training

BLANK SLATE

A young puppy's mind is like a blank slate or perhaps a newly formatted computer disk. What you teach your Poodle puppy in his early months will have bearing on his behavior for the rest of his life. For example, it's not usually a problem if your tiny Toy Poodle jumps up on people, but what if your large Standard Poodle jumps up on the neighborhood kids? That could be traumatic! Therefore, it's important to have a picture of what your Poodle will grow up to be.

A baby Poodle's mind is a blank slate. Teach your puppy now what you want him to know for the rest of his life.

HOUSEHOLD RULES

As previously mentioned, start teaching your Poodle puppy the household rules as soon as possible. Your eight- to ten-week-old puppy is not too young to learn, and by starting early, you can prevent him from acquiring bad habits.

When deciding what rules you want him to learn, look at your Poodle puppy not as the baby he is now, but as the adult he will grow up to be. Are you going to want him up on the furniture when he's grown up? A Toy Poodle may be welcome on the furniture, but you may not want that big, long-legged Standard Poodle stretched out on the sofa. Do you want him to jump up on people? Given their own way, all Poodles jump up. Do you want him to do that to the neighbor's children or to your grandmother?

Some rules that you may want to institute could include teaching your Poodle that jumping up on people is not allowed, that he must behave when guests come to the house, that he should stay out of the kitchen, that he should leave the trash cans alone, and that he should chew only on his toys.

Teaching your Poodle puppy these rules is not difficult. Be very clear with your corrections. When he does something wrong, correct him in a deep, firm tone of voice, "No jump!" When he does something right, use a higher-pitched tone of voice, "Good boy to chew on your toy!" Again, you must be very clear. To a puppy, something is either right or wrong—there are no shades of gray in between.

ACCEPTING THE LEASH

Learning to accept the leash can be difficult for some puppies. If your Poodle puppy learns to dislike the leash as a young puppy, he may continue to resent it for many years. However, if he learns that the leash is a key to more exciting things, he will welcome it.

Soon after you bring your puppy home, put a soft buckle collar on his neck. Make sure it's loose enough to come over his head in case he becomes tangled up in something. Give him a day or two to get used to the collar. Then, when you are going to be close by and can supervise him, snap the leash onto the collar and let him drag it behind him. As he walks around, he'll get used to the feeling of the leash pulling and

While your puppy is getting used to his collar and leash, keep the walks short. Use treats to get the dog to walk forward, and if he balks, never drag him to you. Instead, happily call him to come to you.

Photo by Isabelle Francais

IF YOUR PUPPY BALKS

If your puppy balks, do not use the leash to drag him to you. This will cause him to dig his feet in and apply the brakes. Instead, kneel down, open your arms wide, and encourage him to come to you, "Hey, Sweetie, here! Good boy!" When he dashes to your lap, praise him and tell him what a wonderful puppy he is. Then try the exercise again.

tugging.

After two or three short sessions like this, you can begin to teach your puppy to follow you on the leash. Have a few pieces of an easily chewable, soft treat that your puppy enjoys. Hold the leash in one hand and the treats in another. Show him the treat and back away a few steps as you tell your puppy, "Let's go! Good boy!" When he follows you a few steps, praise him and give him the treat. Poodle puppies are usually very motivated by food and when he learns that a treat is being offered, he should follow you with no problem.

Repeat this two or three times and then stop for this training session. Reward your puppy by giving him a tummy rub or by throwing him a ball.

After two or three training sessions like this, make it more challenging by backing away slowly, quickly, or by making turns. If he gets confused or balks, make it simple until he willingly follows you again.

INTRODUCING THE CAR

Many puppies are afraid of the car because they associate it with leaving their mother and littermates. The car also takes them to the veterinarian's office, where a stranger in a white coat pokes and prods them. You don't want this fear of the car to grab hold, so help

If your puppy is afraid of the car, reintroduce him to it slowly, using treats to convince him that it's not so bad after all.

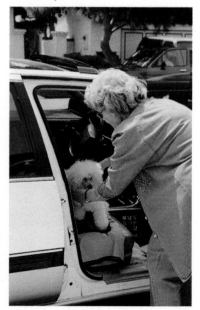

your puppy understand that riding in the car is great fun and safe.

Start by putting your puppy in the car and handing him a treat. As soon as he finishes the treat, take him out of the car and walk away. Repeat this simple exercise several times a day for a few days. The next step is to put him in the car, give him a treat, and let him explore the car for a few minutes. After he has sniffed around for a bit, give him another treat, let him eat it, take him out of the car, and walk away. Continue this training for a week or two, depending upon how nervous your puppy is in the car.

When your puppy is

expecting a treat in the car, put his crate in the car and strap it down securely. Place your puppy in his crate, give him a treat, and then start the car's engine. Drive the car up and down the driveway a few times. Stop the engine, give your puppy a treat, and let him out of his crate.

The next time, drive down

End all training sessions with success and praise so that your Poodle will be motivated to work hard the next time you train together.

Photo by Isabelle Francais

the street and eventually around the block. Increase the distances and times of the drives very gradually. Keep in mind that you want your puppy to expect only good things in the car.

SOCIAL HANDLING

Your Poodle puppy cannot take care of himself. You're responsible for brushing, combing, and bathing him, checking his feet for cuts and scrapes, and cleaning his ears. Because a puppy doesn't understand why you need to groom him, he may struggle when you try to care for him. This social handling exercise will help teach your puppy how to accept your care.

Sit on the floor and have

Even the smallest Poodle puppies must be groomed, so don't let cumbersome grooming tools stop you from getting the job done. There are compact, lightweight tools available. Photo courtesy of Wahl, USA.

your puppy lie down between your legs. He can either lie on his back or on his side. Start by giving him a slow, easy tummy rub to relax him. If your movements are fast and vigorous, you'll make him want to play. If he starts to struggle, tell him calmly, "Easy, be still." Restrain him gently if you need to do so.

When your puppy is relaxed, start giving him a massage. Begin at his neck and ears, gently rubbing all around the base of each ear and working down the neck to the shoulders. Continue massaging his body, checking for cuts,

---

RELAX!

You can also use the social handling exercise to relax your puppy when he's overstimulated. If you let him in from the back-yard and he's full of Poodle energy, don't chase him down or try to correct him. Instead, sit down on the floor and invite him to join you. (Use a treat if you need some extra incentive.) Once he comes to you, lay him down and begin the massage. He will relax and calm down and in the process, you are giving him the attention that he needs from you.

scratches, lumps, bumps, bruises, fleas, ticks, or any other problems that need to be taken care of. Once your puppy feels comfortable being handled, you can clean his ears, wash out his eyes, or trim his toenails.

Poodles need to be groomed on a daily basis. Make grooming more enjoyable for your Poodle by keeping the sessions short and sweet and interspersed with tummy rubs and massages. If the grooming process is difficult now, it will be for your puppy's entire life.

HOUSETRAINING

One of the most common methods of housetraining a puppy is paper training. A puppy is taught to relieve himself on newspapers and then, at some point, is retrained to go outside. Paper training teaches a puppy to relieve himself inside the house, but is that really what you want your Poodle to learn? Owners of some very small Toy Poodles may want their dog to relieve himself inside on papers or in a cat litter box. If that's the case, then train your Poodle to go on the papers. However, if your eventual goal is to have your dog relieve himself outside, start the process while he's a puppy.

Teach your Poodle the things that you want him to know as a puppy and as an adult. Take him outside to the place where you want him to relieve himself and tell him, "Sweetie, go potty." (Use any word you'll be comfortable saying.) Praise him when he finishes.

Don't just open the door and send your puppy outside. How will you know that he has relieved himself? Go outside with him so that you can teach him the command and praise him when he performs properly.

It's not a problem if he doesn't relieve himself when you take him outside. Simply put him back in his crate for a little while and take him outside later. Do not let him run around the house if he has not relieved himself outside.

Successful housetraining is based upon setting your Poodle puppy up for success rather than failure. Keep accidents to a minimum and praise him when he relieves himself in the proper place.

Establish a Routine

Poodles, like many other dogs, are creatures of habit and thrive on a routine. Housetraining is much easier if there is a set routine for eating, eliminating, playing, walking, training, and sleeping. The following is an example of a workable schedule:

• **6:00 am**—Dad wakes up and takes the puppy outside. After the puppy relieves himself, Dad praises him and brings him inside. Dad fixes the puppy's breakfast, offers him water, and then sends him out in the backyard while he takes his shower.

• **7:00 am**—Mom goes outside to play with the puppy for a few minutes before getting ready for work. Just before she leaves, she brings the puppy inside, puts him in his crate, and gives him a treat.

• **11:00 am**—A dog-loving neighbor who is retired comes over. He lets the puppy out of his crate and takes him outside. The neighbor is familiar with the puppy's training, so he praises the puppy when he relieves himself. He throws the ball for the puppy, pets him, and cuddles him. When the puppy is worn out, he puts him back in his crate, and gives him a treat.

• **3:00 pm**—Daughter comes home from school and takes the puppy outside. She throws the ball for the puppy and takes him for a walk. When they get back, she brings the puppy

> ### PUNISHMENT
> Do not try to housetrain your puppy by correcting him for relieving himself in the house. If you scold him, you are not teaching him where he needs to relieve himself. Instead, you are teaching him that you think going potty is wrong. Because he has to go, he will then become sneaky about it, and you will find puddles and piles in strange places. Don't concentrate on correcting him, emphasize the praise for going potty in the right place

inside to her bedroom while she does her homework.

• **6:00 pm**—Mom takes the puppy outside to go potty, praises him, and then feeds him dinner.

• **8:00 pm**—After Daughter plays with the puppy, she brushes him and then takes him outside to go potty.

• **11:00 pm**—Dad takes the puppy outside to go potty before bed.

The schedule you set up will have to work with your normal routine and lifestyle. Keep in mind that your Poodle puppy should not remain in the crate for longer than three to four hours at a time, except during the night. In addition, the puppy will need to relieve himself after waking up, after eating,

Photo by Isabelle Francais

Enlisting a neighbor's or professional petsitter's assistance with your housetraining routine may help speed the process along.

after playtime, and every three to four hours in between.

Limit the Puppy's Freedom

Many puppies do not want to take the time to go outside to relieve themselves because everything exciting happens in the house. After all, that's where all the family members are. If your Poodle puppy is like this, you will find him sneaking off somewhere—behind the sofa or to another room—to relieve himself. By limiting the puppy's freedom, you can prevent some of these mistakes. Close bedroom doors

Indoor housetraining accidents are always the owner's fault, not the puppy's. The dog is only doing what comes naturally—it is up to his owner to let him out regularly and show him where to relieve himself.

Photo by Isabelle Francais

THERE ARE NO ACCIDENTS

If the puppy relieves himself in the house, it is not his fault, it's yours. An accident means that the puppy was not supervised well enough or he wasn't taken outside in time. The act of relieving himself is very natural to the puppy and the idea that certain areas are not acceptable is foreign to him. His instincts tell him to keep his bed clean, but that's all. It's your responsibility to show your puppy the proper place to relieve himself.

and put baby gates across hallways to keep him contained. If you can't keep an eye on him, put him in his crate or outside.

CRATE TRAINING

By about five weeks of age, most puppies are starting to toddle away from their mom and littermates to relieve themselves. Although this instinct helps to keep the bed clean, using a crate makes the housetraining process easier.

A crate is a plastic or wire travel cage that you can use as your Poodle's bed. Many new Poodle owners shudder at the thought of putting their puppy in a cage, often comparing it to putting a child in jail. However, a puppy is not a child and has different needs and instincts.

Puppies like to curl up in small dark places, such as under a coffee table or chair.

Because it's a Poodle puppy's instinct to keep his bed clean, being confined in the crate will help him develop more bowel and bladder control. When he is confined for gradually extended periods of time, he will hold his wastes to avoid soiling his bed. It is your responsibility to make sure that he isn't left in the crate for too long.

The crate will also be your Poodle puppy's place of refuge. If he's tired, hurt, or sick, allow him to go back to his crate to sleep or hide. If he's

These six-week-old Poodles already have an instinct to keep their bed clean by relieving themselves elsewhere. The crate training technique makes use of that natural tendency.

Photo by Isabelle Francais

PATIENCE, PATIENCE, AND MORE PATIENCE

Poodle puppies need time to develop bowel and bladder control. Establish a routine that works well for both of you and stick to it. Give your puppy enough time to learn what you want and time to grow up. If you stick to the schedule, your puppy will progress. However, don't let success go to your head. A few weeks without a mistake doesn't mean that your Poodle puppy is completely housetrained; it means your routine is working. Allowing your puppy too much freedom early on will result in problems.

overstimulated or excited, put him back in his crate to calm down.

Because the crate physically confines the puppy, it can also prevent some unwanted behaviors, such as destructive chewing or raiding the trash cans. When you cannot supervise the puppy or when you leave the house, put him in his crate to prevent him from getting into trouble.

Introducing the Crate

Introduce your puppy to the crate by propping open the door and tossing a treat inside. As you do this, tell your puppy, "Go to bed!" When he goes

Photo by Isabelle Francais

When housetraining your Poodle, never send him outside by himself to eliminate. Go out with him so that you can show him where to go and praise him when he is through.

inside to get the treat, let him investigate the crate and come and go as he wishes. Once he's comfortable with that, offer him his next meal in the crate. As soon as he's in, close the door behind him and let him out when he's through eating. Offer several meals in the same fashion to show your puppy that the crate is a pretty neat place.

After your Poodle puppy is used to going in and out of the crate for treats and meals, start feeding him in his normal place again and go back to offering a treat for going into the crate. Tell him, "Sweetie, go to bed" and then give him his treat.

Don't let your puppy out of the crate for a temper tantrum. If he starts crying, screaming, throwing himself at the door, or scratching at the door, correct him verbally, "No, quiet!" or simply close the door to the room and walk away. If you let him out after a tantrum, you will be teaching him that temper tantrums equal satisfaction. Instead, let him out when he's quiet and you're ready.

Crate Location

The ideal place for the crate is in your bedroom, within arm's reach of the bed. This will give your poodle eight uninterrupted hours with you while you do nothing but sleep. In these busy times, that is quality time.

Having you nearby will give your Poodle puppy a feeling of security, whereas exiling him to the laundry room or backyard will isolate him. He will be more apt to cry, whine, chew destructively, or get into other kinds of trouble because of loneliness and fear.

Having the crate close to you at night will save you some wear and tear, too. If he needs to go outside during the night (and he may need to for a few weeks), you will hear him whine, and you can let him out before he has an accident. If he's restless or bored, you can rap on the top of his crate and tell him to be quiet without getting out of bed.

TIMING AGAIN

Do you walk your dog when he has to go potty? Many dog owners that live in condos and apartments have to take their dogs for a walk in order for them to relieve themselves. These dogs often learn that the walk is over once they go potty, so they hold it as long as possible. To avoid this trap, encourage your puppy to relieve himself right away, praise him, and then continue the walk.

The Basic
OBEDIENCE
Commands

THE TEACHING PROCESS

Although Poodles are very intelligent dogs, you cannot simply tell your Poodle to do something and expect him to understand your verbal language. The training process begins with teaching your dog that certain words have meanings and that you would like him to follow your directions.

Show Your Dog

First of all, you want to show your dog what you want him to do and that there is a word associated with that action or position. For example, when teaching him to sit, you can help him into position as you tell him, "Sweetie, sit." Even if you helped him into that position, follow the action with praise, "Good boy to sit."

You will follow a similar pattern when teaching your dog most new things. If you want him off the sofa, you can tell him, "Sweetie, off the furniture," as you take him by the collar and pull him off. When he's off the furniture, tell

Don't use corrections that are too harsh or unfair. Your dog will resent it, and your training will not progress.

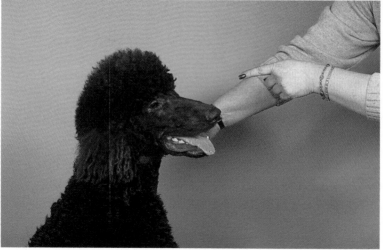

Photo by Isabelle Francais

Photo by Isabelle Francais

The teaching process is very important to successful training. First, show your Poodle what you want him to do, then praise him when he does it right. Correct your dog only when he deliberately disobeys.

him, "Good boy to get off the furniture."

Praise

Praise your dog every time he does something right, even if you helped him do it. Your Poodle will pay more attention to his behavior and try harder if he is praised for his efforts. However, don't praise him when it's undeserved. Poodles are very intelligent dogs and will quickly figure it out. Instead, praise him enthusiastically when he makes an effort and performs the correct behavior.

Correct

Do not correct your dog until he understands exactly what you want him to do. After he understands the command but chooses not to obey it, correct him verbally "Sweetie, no!" or with a quick snap and release of the collar. Don't overcorrect your dog. Less corrections are usually more effective as long as he is responding.

Your Timing

The timing of your praise, corrections, and interruptions is very important. Praise your dog as he's performing the desired behavior and correct him only

USE INTERRUPTIONS

Interrupt your dog's inappropriate behavior as you see it happen. If your dog is walking by the kitchen trash can and turns to sniff it, interrupt him, "Leave it alone!" If you tell him to sit and he obeys you, but then starts to get up, interrupt him, "No! Sit." By interrupting him, you can stop incorrect behavior before it progresses.

Interruptions and corrections alone will not teach your Poodle because they are used to stop—at that moment—undesirable behavior or actions. Your Poodle learns much more when you reward good behavior. Stop the behavior you don't want, but lavishly praise the actions you want to continue.

when he makes a mistake. For example, interrupt him as he starts to stick his nose into the trash can, not after. If your timing is slow, he may not understand what you are trying to teach him.

Be Fair

Poodles resent corrections that are too harsh or unfair. They will show their discontent by refusing to work, by planting themselves and not moving, or by fighting back. Some Poodles will even show signs of depression if you continue to enforce a harsh training method.

THE COME COMMAND

The come command is one of the most important commands that your Poodle needs to learn. Not only is this command important in your daily routine, but it could also be a life saver someday, especially if he decides to dash toward the street when a car is coming. You can use two different techniques to teach your dog the come command.

With a Treat

The first technique uses a sound stimulus and a treat to teach your Poodle the come command. Take a small plastic container (such as a margarine tub) and put a handful of dry

dog food in it. Put the lid on and shake it to make a rattling sound.

Have the shaker in one hand and some tasty dog treats in the other. Shake the container, and as your Poodle looks at it, ask him, "Sweetie, cookie?" Use the word that he already knows for a treat. I use the word cookie but you can use anything

The come command is the first command you should teach your Poodle. Use a treat, a verbal command, and a rattling shaker to train your dog to respond enthusiastically.

he already understands. When you say cookie, pop a treat in his mouth. Repeat the process. Shake, shake, "Sweetie, cookie?" and pop a treat in his mouth. The sound of the container, your verbal question, and the treat are all becoming associated in his mind. Do this several times a day for several days.

The next step is to replace the word "cookie" with the word "come." Shake the container, say "Sweetie, come!" and pop a treat in his mouth. You are rewarding him even though he didn't actually come

Photo by Isabelle Francais

Don't worry about using treats at first to aid in your training. When your Poodle is well trained, he will obey your commands whether you have a treat or not.

USING A SOUND STIMULUS

Do you remember those silent dog whistles that used to be advertised in comic books? There was nothing magical about them, except that they were so high-pitched that only dogs could hear them. The container used for teaching the come command works on the same principal as the silent dog whistles. A sound stimulus is used to teach the dog to pay attention to the sound of the shaker. The noise of the shaker means that he's going to get a treat, which makes coming to you more exciting. Your dog will be more likely to obey the come command (especially when there are distractions) if he's excited about it.

to you. However, you are teaching him that the sound of the shaker now equals the word come, and he still gets the treat. This is another important lesson. Practice this several times a day for several days.

When your Poodle is happy to hear the shaker and drooling to get a treat, start calling him from across the room. Shake the container as you say, "Sweetie, come!" When he dashes to you, continue to give him a treat as you praise him, "Good boy to come!" Practice this up and down the hallway, inside and outside, and across the backyard. Make it fun by keeping up with the treats and the verbal praise.

The Come with a Long Line

The second method used to teach your dog the come command uses a long leash or a piece of clothesline rope. You should have a line at least 30 feet in length, because Poodles are athletic and fast. Fasten the line to your Poodle's collar and then let him go play. When he is distracted by something, call him to come, "Sweetie, come!" If he responds and comes right away, praise him.

If he doesn't respond right away, do not call him again. Pick up the line, back away from him, and make him come to

To teach the come command using a long line, fasten the line to your Poodle's collar, then call him to come. If he ignores you, use the line to drag him toward you.

you. Do not give him a verbal correction at this time because he may associate it with coming to you. Instead, simply make him come to you, even if you have to drag him in with the line.

Let him go again and repeat the entire exercise. Make sure that you always praise him when he does decide to come to you. If he is really distracted, use the shaker and treats along with the long line, especially in the early stages of the training. You can always wean him from the treats later. Your main objective is to teach your Poodle the come command.

Don't allow your Poodle to have freedom off the leash

Don't allow your Poodle to run around off leash until he is old enough to handle it. The athletic, agile Poodle can fly away from you before you've even noticed he's gone.

Photo by Isabelle Francais

CONTROL COMMANDS
The sit, down, and stay exercises are called control commands because your dog learns how to stay still and control himself. These commands can be hard for active dogs, but they are absolutely necessary.

until he is well trained and can handle the responsibility. Many owners let their dog off leash much too soon, and as a result, the dog learns bad habits. Each time your dog learns that he can ignore you or run away from you, it reinforces the fact that he can. Instead, let him run around and play while dragging the long line. That way you can always regain control when you need it.

SIT AND RELEASE
The sit command is the foundation for everything else your Poodle will learn. Not only does he learn how to sit still, he also learns how to control himself and that there are consequences to his actions.

The sit command is also a good alternative action for problem behavior. Your Poodle cannot sit still and jump on you at the same time. Learning how to sit still for praise can replace jumping up on people for attention. He can't knock his

SIT, PLEASE!

Once your Poodle understands the sit command and is responding well, start having him sit for things that he wants. For example, have him sit before you hook his leash to his collar before a walk or before you give him a treat.

food bowl out of your hand if he's sitting, waiting patiently for his dinner. You can fasten his leash to his collar more easily if he's sitting. This is a practical, useful command.

There are two basic methods of teaching your Poodle how to sit. Some dogs have more success with one technique than the other, so try both, and see which works better for your Poodle.

Hold his leash in your left hand and have some treats in your right hand. Tell your Poodle, "Sweetie, sit!" as you move your right hand (with the treats) from his nose over his head and toward his tail. He will lift his head to watch your hand. As his head goes up and back, his hips will go down. As he sits, praise him, "Good boy to sit!" and give him a treat. Pet him while he's in the sitting position.

When you are ready for him to get up, tap him on the shoulder as you tell him,

"Release!" Each exercise needs a beginning and an end. The sit command is the beginning and the release command tells him that he is done and can now move. If he doesn't get up on his own, use your hands on his collar to walk him forward.

If your Poodle is too excited by the treats to think, put them away. Tell him to sit as you place one hand under his chin on the front of the neck and slide the other hand down his hips to tuck under his back legs. Gently shape him into a sitting position as you give him the command, "Sweetie, sit." Praise him and release him.

If your dog is wiggly as you teach him this exercise, keep your hands on him. If he pops up, interrupt that action using a

When you teach the sit command, gently shape your Poodle's hips into a seated position if necessary.

Photo by Robert Pearcy

deep, firm tone of voice, "Be still!" When he responds and stops wiggling, praise him quietly and gently.

DOWN

The down command also teaches self-control. It is hard for many energetic, bouncy young Poodles to control their own actions, but it is a lesson that they all must learn. Practicing the down exercise teaches your Poodle to lie down and be still.

Start with your Poodle in a sitting position. Rest one hand gently on his shoulder and have a treat in the other hand. Let him smell the treat and then tell him, "Sweetie, down." Put the treat on the ground in front of his paws. As he follows the treat down, use your hand on

ONE COMMAND

Don't keep repeating any command. The command is not "Sit! Sit, sit, sit, please sit. SIT!!" If you give repeated commands for the sit, your Poodle will assume that carries on to everything else. Tell him once to sit and then help him do it.

his shoulders to encourage him to lie down. Praise him, give him the treat, and then have him hold the position for a moment. Release him in the same way you did from the sit. Pat him on the shoulder, tell him "Release!" and let him get up.

If your dog looks at the treat as you make the signal but doesn't follow the treat to the ground, simply scoop his front legs up and forward as you lay him down. The rest of the

For the down command, begin with the dog in the sit position, then bring a treat down to the ground in front of him as you give the verbal command. If he doesn't lie down, simply scoop his front legs out from under him to help him learn.

exercise is the same.

As your poodle learns what the down command means, you can have him hold it for a few minutes longer before you release him, but do not step away from him yet. Stay next to him and if he's wiggly, keep a hand on his shoulder to help him stay in the down position.

Once a day, have your Poodle lie down and before you release him, roll him over for a tummy rub. He will enjoy the tummy rub, relax a little, and learn to enjoy the down position. This is especially important for young Poodles that want to do anything but lie down and hold still.

STAY

When your Poodle understands both the sit and down commands, you can introduce him to the stay exercise. You want to convey to your Poodle that the word stay means hold still. When your dog is sitting and you tell him to stay, you want him to remain in the sitting position until you go back to him and release him. When you tell him to stay while he's lying down, you want him to remain lying down until you go back to him to release him from that position. Eventually, he will be

> ### BE CLEAR
> Make sure that you make it very clear to your dog what you want him to do. Remember, something is either completely right or wrong to your dog; it's not partly right or wrong. Be fair with your commands, your praise, and your corrections.

able to hold the sit position for several minutes and the down for even longer.

Start by having your Poodle sit. With the leash in your left hand, use it to put a slight bit of pressure backward (toward his tail) as you tell him, "Sweetie, stay." At the same time, use your right hand to give your dog a hand signal that will mean stay—an open-handed gesture with the palm toward your dog's face. Take one step away and at the same time, release the pressure on the leash.

If your dog moves or gets up, tell him "No!" so that he knows he made a mistake. Put him back into position and repeat the exercise. After a few seconds, go back to him and praise him. Don't let him move from position until you release him. Use the same process to teach the stay in the down position.

With the stay command, you always want to go back to your

Your Poodle should learn to obey the stay command in both the sit and down positions.

Poodle to release him. Don't release him from a distance or call him to come from the stay. If you do either of these, your dog will be much less reliable on the stay. He will continue to get up from the stay because you will have taught him to do exactly that. When teaching the stay, you want your Poodle to learn that stay means hold that position until you come back to release him.

As your Poodle learns the stay command, you can gradually increase the time you ask him to hold it. However, if your dog is making a lot of mistakes, you are either asking him to hold it too long or he doesn't understand the

The stay command is one of the most important commands your dog will learn. Make sure that your dog is as reliable on the stay as this little Poodle.

USING THE STAY COMMAND

You can use the stay command around the house. For example, in the evening while you're watching a favorite television show, have your Poodle lie down at your feet while you sit on the sofa. Give him a toy to chew on and tell him, "Sweetie, stay." Have him do a down/stay when your guests visit so he isn't jumping all over them. Have him lie down and stay while the family is eating so he isn't begging for food under the table. There are many practical uses for the stay command. Look at your normal routine and see where this command can work for you.

---

command yet. In either case, go back and reteach the exercise from the beginning.

Increase the distance from your dog very gradually, too. Again, if your dog is making many mistakes, you're moving away too quickly. Teach everything very gradually.

When your Poodle understands the stay command but chooses not to do it, you need to let him know that the command is not optional. Many young wiggly Poodles want to do anything but hold still. Correct excess movement first with your voice, "No! Be still! Stay!" and if that doesn't stop

For the watch me command, take a treat in your right hand from his nose up to your chin as you say, "Watch me!"

to your chin. When his eyes follow the treat in your hand, and he looks at your face, praise him, "Good boy to watch me!" and give him the treat. Release him from the sit. Repeat it two or three times and end the training session.

Because this is hard for young, bouncing Poodles, practice the exercise first at home when there are few distractions. Make sure that your dog knows it well before you take him outside and try to practice it with distractions. However, once he knows it well inside, you'll need to try it with distractions. Take him out in the front yard (on leash, of course) and tell him to watch you. If he ignores you, take his chin in your left hand (the treat is in the right) and hold it so that he looks at your face. Praise him even though you are helping him do it.

When he will watch you outside with some distractions, then move on to the next step. Have him sit in front of you and tell him to watch you as you take a few steps backward. Praise him when he does. Try it again. When he can follow you six or seven steps and watch you at the same time, make it more challenging—back up and turn to the left or right or back

the excess movement, use a verbal correction with a snap and release of the leash. When he does control himself, praise him enthusiastically.

WATCH ME

The watch me exercise teaches your Poodle to ignore distractions and pay attention to you. This is particularly useful when you're out in public and your dog is distracted by children playing or dogs barking behind a fence.

Start by having your Poodle sit in front of you. Have a treat in your right hand. Let him sniff the treat and then tell him, "Sweetie, watch me!" as you take the treat from his nose up

up faster. Praise him when he continues to watch you.

HEEL

You want your Poodle to learn that heel means "walk by my left side, with your neck and shoulders by my left leg, and maintain that position." Ideally, your Poodle should maintain that position as you walk slow, fast, turn corners, or weave in and out through a crowd.

To start, practice a "watch me" exercise to get your dog's attention. Back away from him and encourage him to watch you. When he is, simply turn your body as you are backing up so that your dog ends up on your left side. Continue walking.

If done correctly, you and your dog end up walking forward together, with him on your left side.

Let's walk it through in slow motion. Sit your dog in front of you and do a "watch me." Back away from your dog and encourage him to follow you. When he's watching you, back up toward your left and continue turning in that direction so that you and your dog end up walking forward together. Your dog should end up on your left side (or you should end up on your dog's right side).

If your dog starts to pull forward, simply back away from him and encourage him to

A retractable leash is a useful tool when you teach the heel exercise to your Poodle. Retractable leashes provide freedom for the dog while allowing the owner complete control. Leashes are available in a wide variety of lengths for all breeds of dog. Photo courtesy of Flexi-USA, Inc.

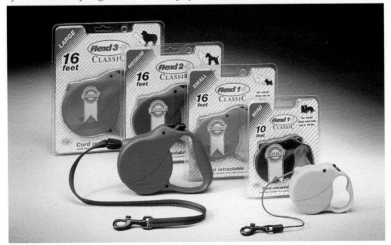

follow you. If you need to do so, use the leash with a snap-and-release motion to make the dog follow you. Praise him when he does.

Don't hesitate to go back and forth if you need to do so. In fact, sometimes this can be the most effective way to get your dog's attention on you.

When your dog is walking nicely and paying attention to you, start eliminating the backing away. Begin the heel with your Poodle sitting by your left side. Tell him, "Sweetie, watch me! Heel," and start walking. When he's walking nicely with you, praise him.

USE IT OR LOSE IT!

The best way to make this training work for you and your Poodle is to practice. Training is for your everyday life. Incorporate it into your daily routine. Have your Poodle sit before you feed him. Have him lie down and stay while you eat. Have him sit and stay at the gate while you take the trash cans out. Have him do a down/stay when guests come over. Use these commands as part of your life. They will work much better that way.

However, if he gets distracted or starts to pull, simply back away from him again.

Your Poodle should learn that heel means that he should walk by your left side, with his neck and shoulders by your left leg, and maintain that position. This is a big lesson, but it will make walks much more enjoyable.

All About
FORMAL
Training

WHY IS TRAINING IMPORTANT?

You probably decided to add a Poodle to your family because you wanted a companion, a friend, a protector, and a confidant. You may have wanted a dog to go for walks with you and to take jogs with, or maybe you wanted your children to have the same kind of relationship with a dog that you remember from your childhood. However, to do any of these things, your Poodle will need training. Many dog owners won't admit that. "He does everything I ask," they say. Yet when asked specific questions about their Poodle's behavior, the answer changes. A trained Poodle won't jump up on people, dash out the open door, or raid the trash can.

Dog owners benefit from training by learning how to motivate their Poodle. They also learn how to prevent problem behavior and how to correct mistakes that do happen.

Dog training entails much more than learning the traditional sit, down, stay, and come commands. It means teaching your Poodle that he's living in your house, not his. You can set some rules and expect him to follow them. It will not turn your Poodle into a robot, but instead teach him to look at you in a new light. Training will cause you to look at him differently, too. It's not something that you do to your Poodle, it's something you do together.

To be the best pet he can be, your dog will require training. A well-trained Poodle won't jump on people or misbehave in other ways.

Photo by Isabelle Francais

GOALS FOR YOUR POODLE

What do you want training to accomplish? Do you want your Poodle to be calm and well behaved around family members and when he's out in public? Would you like to participate in dog activities and sports? There are an unlimited number of things that you can do with your Poodle. Decide what you would like to do and then find a training program to help you achieve those goals. As you start training, talk to your trainer so she can guide you in the right direction.

FINDING AN INSTRUCTOR OR TRAINER

When trying to find an instructor or trainer, word-of-mouth referrals are probably the best place to start. Although anyone can place an advertisement in the newspaper or yellow pages, the ad itself is no guarantee of quality or expertise. However, satisfied customers will have well-behaved dogs and be glad to tell you where they received instruction.

Have you admired a neighbor's well-behaved Poodle? Ask them where they went for training. Call your veterinarian, local pet store, or groomer and ask who they recommend. Make notes about each referral. What did people like and dislike about this trainer?

Once you have a list of

Before embarking on formal training, decide what you want to accomplish. Do you want your dog to be a well-mannered housepet? An athlete? A champion show dog? Or all of the above?

Photo by Tara Darling

referrals, start calling the instructors and ask a few questions. How long has she been teaching classes? You will want someone with experience so that she can handle any situation that may arise. However, experience alone is not the only qualification. Some people that have been training for years are still using the same teaching method and haven't progressed.

Ask the instructor what she thinks of the breed. Ideally, she should be knowledgeable about the breed, knowing what makes them tick and how to train them. If she doesn't like the breed, go elsewhere.

Ask the instructor to explain her training methods. Does her approach sound like something you would be comfortable with? Ask if there are alternative methods used, because not every dog will respond the same way to a training program. Every instructor should have a backup plan.

Does the instructor belong to any professional organizations? The National Association of Dog Obedience Instructors (NADOI) and the Association of Pet Dog Trainers (APDT) are two of the more prominent groups. Both of

Photo by Isabelle Francais

Word-of-mouth referrals are the best way to find a good dog trainer or instructor. You may wish to ask a neighbor where her nicely behaved Poodle received training.

these organizations publish regular newsletters to share information, techniques, new developments, and more. Instructors that belong to these organizations are more likely to be up-to-date on training techniques and styles, as well as information about specific dog breeds.

Also, make sure that the instructor will be able to help you achieve your goals. For example, if you want to compete in obedience trials, the instructor should have experience in that field and knowledge of the rules and regulations concerning that competition.

After talking to several trainers or instructors, ask them if you can observe their training or classes. If someone says that you can't watch their class, then cross them off your list. There should be no reason why you cannot attend one class to see if you will be comfortable with an instructor and her style of teaching. As you watch the class, see how she handles the dogs and ask yourself if you would let her handle your dog. How does she relate to the dogs? Are they relaxed and do they look like they're having a good time? Are they paying attention to the instructor?

After talking to several instructors or trainers and observing their classes, you should be able to decide which class you want to attend. If you're still unsure, call the instructors back and ask a few more questions. After all, you are hiring them to provide a service and you must be comfortable with your decision.

TRAINING METHODS

If you talk to 100 different dog trainers (someone who trains dogs) or dog obedience instructors (someone who teaches a dog owner how to train his dog) and ask them how they train, you will get 100 different answers. Any trainer or instructor who has been in the business for any period of time is going to have a method or technique that works best

When you observe a training class, decide if you will be comfortable with the instructor's style of teaching.

Photo by Robert Pearcy

poodles

Photo by Isabelle Francais

Inducive training methods motivate the dog with treats and use few or no corrections.

for her. Each method will be based on the trainer's personality, teaching techniques, experience, and philosophy regarding dogs and dog training. Any given method may work wonderfully for one trainer, but fail terribly for another.

Because there are so many different techniques, styles, and methods, choosing a particular instructor may be difficult. It is important to understand some of the different methods so that you can make a reasonable decision.

Compulsive Training

Compulsive training is a method of training that forces the dog to behave. A correction-based training style that sometimes uses forceful corrections, compulsive training is often used in conjunction with law enforcement. Hard-driving, strong-willed dogs, such as military dogs, are quite effective in this method of training.

Many dog owners do not like compulsive training because they feel that it's too rough. It is rarely the right type of training technique for a Poodle.

Inducive Training

This training is exactly the opposite of compulsive training. Instead of being forced to do something, the dog is induced or motivated toward proper behavior. Depending upon the instructor, there are few or no corrections used. Inducive training works very well for most puppies, nonaggressive dogs, and owners who dislike corrections of any kind.

Unfortunately, inducive training is not always the right technique for all Poodles. Many Poodles will take advantage of the lack of corrections or discipline. Some very intelligent dogs that have dominating personalities (including some Poodles) look upon the lack of discipline as a weakness on your part, and will then set their own rules accordingly. Unfortunately, those rules may not be suitable.

Somewhere in the Middle

The majority of trainers and instructors use a training method that is somewhere in between both of these techniques. An inducive method is used when possible, while corrections are used when needed. Obviously, the range can be vast, with some trainers leaning more toward corrections and others using as few as possible.

In a group class, your Poodle must learn to behave around real-world distractions. You will also enjoy the support of other class members who, like you, are experiencing the joys and frustrations of dog training.

GROUP CLASSES OR PRIVATE LESSONS?

There are benefits and drawbacks to both group classes and private lessons. In group classes, the dog must learn to behave around distractions, specifically the other dogs and people in the class. A group class can work like group therapy for dog owners because they can share the triumphs and the mishaps, as well as encourage and support one another. Many friendships have begun in group training classes.

For some dogs, the drawback to a group class is that distractions make it difficult to concentrate, especially in the beginning of training. For these dogs, a few private lessons may help enough so that the dog can then join a group class later. Dogs with severe behavior problems, especially aggression, should bypass group classes for obvious reasons.

Private lessons—one-on-one training with the owner, dog, and instructor—are also good for people with very busy schedules who may not be able to do any training at all.

PUPPY CLASS

Puppy kindergarten classes consist of obedience training

For some Poodles, one-on-one training lessons are a better choice, especially at first. They are also more convenient for owners with busy schedules.

and socialization and are for puppies between the ages of 10 and 16 weeks. A puppy owner also learns how to prevent problem behaviors from occurring and how to establish household rules.

BASIC OBEDIENCE CLASS

This class is for puppies that have graduated from a puppy class, for puppies over four months of age that have never attended a class, or for adult dogs. In basic obedience class, the dogs and their owners work on basic obedience commands such as sit, down, stay, come,

Photo by Isabelle Francais

Training helps to build a relationship between you and your dog. His excellent behavior will make you happy to have him around, and he will be thrilled with the praise he receives for being such a good dog.

poodles

and heel. Most instructors also spend time discussing problem prevention and problem solving, especially for common problems like jumping on people, barking, digging, and chewing.

DOG SPORTS TRAINING

Some instructors offer training for one or more of the various dog activities. There are classes to prepare you for competition in obedience trials, conformation dog shows, flyball, agility, and schutzhund. Other trainers may offer training for non-competitive activities such as therapy dog work.

BUILDING A RELATIONSHIP

Training helps to build a relationship between you and your dog. This relationship is built on mutual trust, affection, and respect. Training can help your dog become not only your best friend, but a well-behaved and enjoyable companion.

ADVANCED TRAINING

Advanced training classes vary depending upon the instructor. Some offer classes to teach you how to control your dog off leash, some emphasize dog sports, and others may simply continue basic training skills. Ask the instructor what she offers.

Some trainers will help you and your dog prepare for dog sports. This Poodle has mastered the agility bar jump.

Photo by Isabelle Francais

Problem
PREVENTION
and Solving

Poodles are an active, intelligent breed with the curiosity of a cat. Although that mischievous nature can be a lot of fun, it can also get the dogs into trouble. Because Poodles are easily trained, many Poodle owners are flabbergasted when they find that their beloved dog has chewed up the sofa cushion trying to get to something that dropped behind it. Unfortunately, problem behavior can have many causes and finding a solution isn't always easy.

Many of the behaviors that dog owners consider problems—barking, digging, chewing, and jumping up on people—aren't troublesome to your Poodle. In fact, they are very natural behaviors to your dog. For example, dogs dig because the dirt smells good or there's a gopher in the yard. Dogs bark in order to communicate. All of the things that you consider problem behaviors are very natural to your dog. However, most problem behavior can be prevented, controlled, or in some cases, stopped entirely.

TRAINING

Training can play a big part in controlling problem behavior. A fair, upbeat, yet firm training

Poodles are mischievous dogs, and sometimes getting into trouble just comes naturally to them. However, most problem behavior can be prevented, controlled, or stopped entirely.

Photo by Isabelle Francais

program teaches your dog that you are in charge and he is below you in the family pack. The training should also reinforce his concept of you as a kind, calm, and caring leader. In addition, your training skills give you the ability to teach your dog what is acceptable and what is not.

HEALTH PROBLEMS

Some experts feel that 20 percent of all behavior problems are caused by health-related problems. A bladder infection or a gastrointestinal upset commonly causes housetraining accidents. Medications can cause behavior changes, as can thyroid problems, hyperactivity, hormone imbalances, and a variety of other health problems.

If your dog's behavior changes, make an appointment with your veterinarian. Explain how your Poodle has changed his behavior and ask if he could do an exam to find any physical problems possibly attributing to the behavior.

Don't automatically assume that your dog is healthy. If a health problem is causing the behavior change, training or behavior modification won't make it better. Before beginning any training, talk to your veterinarian. Once health problems are ruled out, you can

Proper nutrition is imperative to your dog's health. Veterinarians recommend elevated feeders to help reduce stress on your dog's neck and back muscles. The raised platform also provides better digestion while reducing bloating and gas. Photo courtesy of Pet Zone Products, Ltd.

poodles

start working on correcting the undesirable behavior.

NUTRITION

Nutrition can play a part in causing or solving behavior problems. If your dog is eating a poor-quality food, or if he cannot digest the food that he is being fed, his body may be missing some vital nutrients. If your Poodle is chewing on rocks or wood, eating the stucco off the side of your house, or grazing on the plants in your garden, he may have a nutritional deficiency of some kind.

Some dogs can become hyperactive when fed a high-calorie, high-fat dog food. Other dogs have food allergies that may show up as behavior problems. Poodles can be very prone to food problems, so don't try to save pennies by buying a poor-quality food. If you have any questions about the food your dog is eating, talk to your veterinarian.

PLAY

The key to play is laughter. Researchers know that laughter is wonderful medicine, because it makes you feel better. When you laugh, you feel differently about the world around you.

Laughter and play are very important factors in the

Feed your Poodle properly from the start to prevent behavior problems down the road. Foods for puppies should be nutritionally complete to allow for healthy growth and strong bones. Make sure the puppy food you choose contains only the highest quality ingredients. Photo courtesy of Nutro Products, Inc.

relationship you have with your Poodle. Poodles can be very silly and you should take advantage of that.

Play is a great stress reliever for both you and your Poodle. Make time for play when you are having a hard time at work or after your training sessions.

Sometimes, dogs get into trouble intentionally because they feel ignored. To these dogs, any attention—even negative attention—is better than no attention at all. If you take the time regularly to play with your dog, you can avoid some of these situations.

Exercise

Exercise is just as important for your poodle as it is for you. It works the body, uses up excess energy, relieves stress, and clears the mind. How much exercise is needed depends on your dog and your normal routine. A fast-paced walk might be enough for an older Poodle, but a young, healthy Poodle might need a good run or game of fetch.

PREVENT PROBLEMS FROM HAPPENING

So many of the things that we consider problem behaviors are natural behaviors to your Poodle, but you can prevent

---

BEHAVIOR CHANGES

Kerry Siekmann is a dog trainer. Although Kerry's dog, Spahht, is very well trained, just after she turned seven years old, her behavior began to change drastically. Spahht began to defy Kerry, ignore her directions, and bite her. Because Spahht was normally well behaved, Kerry took her to the veterinarian's for a complete physical and explained that the dog's behavior had changed tremendously. Looking for things that would cause behavior changes, the vet found that Spahht was epileptic (even though Kerry had not yet seen any seizures) and put her on medication. They are now working to balance her medication and Spahht is on the road to good behavior.

---

them from happening. For example, put the trash cans away so that he never discovers they are full of good-tasting surprises. Make sure the kids put their toys away so that your Poodle can't chew them to pieces. It's much easier to prevent a problem from happening than it is to break a bad habit later.

Preventing a problem might require that you fence off the garden, build higher shelves in the garage, or perhaps build your Standard Poodle a dog run.

Don't leave a Miniature or Toy Poodle outside unless the run is covered and the dogs are protected from outside dangers such as coyotes, hawks, or owls.

Part of preventing problems from occurring also requires that you limit your dog's freedom. A young puppy or an untrained dog should never have unsupervised free run of the house, because there is simply too much he can get into. Instead, keep him close to you and close off all rooms. If you can't watch him, put him in his run or out in the backyard.

DEALING WITH SPECIFIC PROBLEMS
Jumping on People

Just about every Poodle owner, at one time or another, has to deal with their dog jumping up on people. That's just the way the breed is. However, you can control the jumping by emphasizing the sit command. If your Poodle is sitting, he can't be jumping up. Teaching him to sit for petting, praise, and treats is important because everything he wants will happen only when he sits.

Use the leash as much as you can to teach your Poodle how to sit. Poodles can be tough to hold onto unless you have something to grab on to. The leash is your

A DOG RUN
A dog run is a safe place for your Poodle to stay while he's unsupervised. In his dog run, he should have protection from the sun and inclement weather, unspillable water, and a few toys. Never scold your dog while he's in the run and don't put him in as punishment. Instead, give him a treat or a toy when you put him in his run. Leave a radio on playing quiet, gentle music.

best training tool. When you come home from work, don't greet your dog until you have a leash and collar in hand. As your dog greets you, slip the leash over his head and help him sit. If he tries to jump, snap and release

A doggie door that leads from the house to a dog run is ideal for your Poodle. The dog run should provide shelter from the weather and a comfortable place to sleep.

Photo by Robert Pearcy

the leash and verbally correct him, "No jump! Sit!" Of course, as with all of your training, praise him when he sits.

When you are out in public, make sure that your Poodle sits before any of your neighbors or friends pet him. Again, use your leash. If he won't sit still, don't let anyone pet him.

The key to correcting bad behavior like jumping up is to make sure that it is not rewarded. If someone pets your Poodle when he jumps up, that behavior has been rewarded. However, the attention he receives when he's sitting will make the command more attractive to him.

Photo by Isabelle Francais

Having a dog that jumps up on people is a problem that most Poodle owners face. You can control this bad behavior by emphasizing the sit command.

Experts say that 20 percent of all behavior problems are caused by health conditions such as poor nutrition. It is important to provide your dog with a nutritionally fortified diet geared toward his stage of life. Look for foods that are naturally preserved, contain no by-products, and are 100% guaranteed. Photo courtesy of Midwestern Pet Foods, Inc.

Digging

If your backyard looks like a military artillery range, you need to concentrate first on preventing this problem from occurring. If you come home from work to find new holes in the lawn or garden, don't correct him then. He probably dug the holes when you first left in the morning and a correction ten hours later won't work.

Instead, build him a dog run and leave him there during the day. If you fence off one side of your yard alongside your house, you might be able to give him an area that is 6 feet wide by 20 feet long, which is a great run. Let him trash this section to his heart's content.

When you can supervise him, let him have free run of the rest of your yard. When he starts to get into trouble, you can use your voice to interrupt him, "Hey! What are you doing? Get out of the garden!"

Making time for exercise, training, and play every day can help a destructive dog use up his energy and stimulate his mind. Most importantly, don't let this dog watch you garden. If you do, he may come to you later with all of those bulbs you planted earlier.

The Barker

Standard and Miniature Poodles are usually not the

Make time for play and exercise every day, in order to channel your Poodle's energy into constructive activities.

Photo by Isabelle Francais

poodles

Photo by Isabelle Francais

It's important to understand why your dog does what he does. Your problem Poodle might simply be lonely and depressed. Poodles need their owner's company to thrive, and some bad behavior may be cured with more positive attention.

problem barkers. Toys have a tendency to be problem barkers. However, any Poodle left alone for many hours each day may find that barking gets him attention, especially if your neighbors yell at him.

Start teaching him to be quiet when you're at home with him. When your Poodle starts barking, tell him, "Quiet!" When he stops, praise him. When he understands what you want, go for a short walk outside, leaving him home. Listen, and when you hear him start barking, come back and correct him. After a few corrections, when he seems to understand, ask your neighbor to come outside to talk. Have the kids out front playing. When your dog barks because he's feeling left out, go back and correct him. Repeat as often as you need to until he understands. You can reduce your dog's emotional need to bark if you make homecomings and departures quiet and low-key. When you leave the house, don't give him hugs and don't tell him repeatedly to be a good dog. These gestures simply make your leaving more emotional. Instead, give him attention an hour or two prior to your leaving and when it's time for you to go, just go. When you come home, ignore your dog for a few minutes and then whisper hello to him. Your Poodle's hearing is very good, but he is going to have to be quiet and still to hear your whispers.

You can also distract your dog when you leave. Take a

If your Poodle barks when you leave the house, try distracting him with a treat or meal as you quietly make your exit.

Photo by Isabelle Francais

Photo by Isabelle Francais

If your dog does escape, don't chase him or yell at him. Call him to you in an enthusiastic tone of voice and then praise him when he listens and comes to you.

poodles

brown paper lunch bag and put a couple of treats in it—maybe a dog biscuit, a piece of carrot, and a slice of apple. Roll the top of the bag over to close it and rip a very tiny hole in the side to give your dog encouragement to get the treats. As you walk out the door or gate, hand the bag to your dog. He will be so busy figuring out where the treats are and how to get them, he'll forget that you are leaving.

Dashing Through Doors and Gates

This is actually one of the easier behavior problems to

Teach your Poodle to sit before going through doors and gates to solve one of the most common behavior problems.

EXTRA HELP

Problem barkers may need extra help, especially if your neighbors are complaining. There are several effective anti-bark collars on the market. All are triggered by the dog's barking and administer a correction to the dog. Some collars make a high-pitched sound, others squirt a whiff of citronella, and some administer a shock. I do not recommend the shock collars for most Poodles because they will panic at this correction. However, the first two collars are quite effective for many dogs. If you have a Toy Poodle, make sure that you get the small-sized collar. There are some on the market made specifically for Toy breed dogs.

solve. Teach your Poodle to sit at all doors and gates. Have him hold that sit until you give him permission to go through or to get up after you have gone through. By teaching him to sit and wait for permission, you will be eliminating the problem.

Start with your dog on leash. Walk him up to a door. Have him sit, tell him to stay, and then open the door in front of him. If he dashes through, use the leash to correct him (snap and release) as you give him a verbal correction, "No! Stay!" Take him back to his original position and do it again. When he can hold the sit at one door, go to another door or gate and repeat the training procedure.

When he can wait while on leash at all doors and gates, then take his leash off and hook up his long line. Fasten one end of the long line to a piece of heavy furniture. Walk him up to the door and tell him to sit and stay. Drop the long line to the ground. With your hands empty, open the door and stand aside. Because your hands are empty (meaning you aren't holding the leash), your Poodle may decide to dash. If he does, the long line will stop him, or you can step on the line. Give him a verbal correction, "No! I said stay!"

Why is your Poodle doing what he's doing? If you can figure that out, you can prevent the problem from happening.

Photo by Isabelle Francais

> **RUNNING FREE**
>
> If your Poodle does make it out through a door or gate, don't chase him. The more you chase him, the better the game, as far as he's concerned. Instead, rattle your shaker. "Sweetie, do you want a cookie? Come!" When he comes back to you, you must praise him for coming even though you may want to wring his neck for dashing through the door. Don't correct him because it will make him avoid you even more the next time it happens.

and bring him back to where he started. Repeat the training session here and at all other doors and gates.

Other Problems

Many behavior problems can be solved or at least controlled using similar techniques. Try to figure out why your Poodle is doing what he's doing. What can you do to prevent the problem from happening? What can you do to teach your dog not to do it? Remember, as with all of your training, a correction alone will not change the behavior; you must also teach your dog the proper behavior.

If you still have some problems or if your dog is showing aggressive tendencies, contact your local dog trainer or behaviorist for some help.

Advanced
TRAINING
and Dog Sports

Poodles are such intelligent dogs that you can always train them to learn new things. If you like spending time with your dog, there is a lot you can do together, such as teaching him hand signals and how to listen to you off leash, or you can participate in a number of different dog activities and sports.

Before you begin any of these exercises or activities, make sure that your Poodle is proficient in all of the basic commands. If he's having trouble with some of the basic commands, go back and review them.

Poodles of all sizes have been successful at dog sports and other advanced training activities. This Toy enjoys agility competitions.

Photo by Isabelle Francais

USING HAND SIGNALS

Dog owners often think of hand signals as something that only very advanced dogs can respond to. Although it does take some training, hand signals are useful for all dog owners. For example, if your dog responds to hand signals, you can give him the signal to go lie down while you're talking on the telephone without having to interrupt your conversation.

HAND SIGNALS

When you start teaching your Poodle hand signals, have a treat in your hand to get his attention. Use the verbal command that he's familiar with to help him understand what you are trying to tell him. As he responds, decrease the verbal command to a whisper and emphasize the hand signal.

In the beginning, the difficult part of teaching hand signals is that your dog may not understand that these movements have any significance. After all, people "talk" with their hands all the time. Dogs learn at an early age to ignore hand and arm movements. Therefore, to make hand signals work, your Poodle needs to watch you. A good treat tucked in the hand making the movement can help.

Come

You want the signal for the come command to be a very broad, easily seen signal, so that your dog can recognize it even if he's distracted by something. This signal will be a wide swing of the right arm, starting with your arm held straight out to your side from the shoulder, horizontal to the ground. The motion will be to bring the hand to your chest following a wide wave, as if you were reaching out to bring your dog to you.

Start teaching the signal by having the come shaker in your right hand. Shake it slightly—even to get your dog's attention—and then complete the signal. Praise your dog when he responds and comes to you.

If he doesn't respond right away, start the signal again. This time, verbally tell him to come as you are making the signal and rattling the shaker. Again, praise him when he comes. Gradually eliminate the verbal command, and when your Poodle is responding well, slowly stop using the shaker.

Down

When you taught your Poodle to lie down using the treat by taking the treat from his nose to the ground in front of his front paws, you were teaching him a hand signal. Granted, he was watching the treat in your hand, but he was also getting used to seeing your hand move. Therefore, switching him over from verbal command to a hand-signal-only command should be easy.

Have your dog sit in front of you. Verbally, tell him "down" as you give him the hand signal for down (with a treat in your hand) just as you did when you were originally teaching it. When he lies down, praise him and then release him. Practice it a few times.

The hand signal for the come command is a wide motion of the arm, first out to the side and then sweeping across the chest.

Photo by Robert Pearcy

Now, give him the signal to go down with a treat in your hand, but do not give him a verbal command. If he lies down, praise him, give him the treat, and release him. If he does not go down, give the leash a slight snap and release down toward the ground—not hard—but just enough to let him know, "Hey! Pay attention!" When he goes down, praise and release him.

When he can follow the signal with no verbal command reliably, make it more challenging. Signal him to lie down when you are across the room from him. Signal him to lie down while you're talking to someone. Signal him to lie down when there are some

Your dog is already familiar with the hand signal for down. Start with him in a seated or standing position, then bring your hand with a treat down to the ground in front of him.

Photo by Robert Pearcy

distractions around him. Remember to praise him enthusiastically when he goes down on the signal.

Sit

If you were able to teach your Poodle to sit using the treat above his nose, you were teaching him to sit using a hand signal. If you had to teach him by shaping him into a sit position, don't worry, you can still teach him a signal.

With your Poodle on leash, hold the leash in your left hand. Have a treat in your right hand. Stand in front of your Poodle and take the treat from his nose upward. At the same time, whisper, "Sit." When he sits, praise him and release him. Try it again. When he is watching your hand and sitting reliably, stop whispering the command and let him follow the signal. If he doesn't sit, jiggle the leash and collar to remind him that something is expected. Again, when he sits, praise him.

Stay

When you taught your Poodle the stay command you used a hand signal—the open-palmed gesture toward his face. This signal is so obvious that your dog will probably do it without any additional training.

Photo by Isabelle Francais

The hand signal for the sit command takes a treat from the Poodle's nose upward. As he leans back to look at the treat, he will automatically sit.

poodles

Have your dog sit or lie down and tell him to stay using only the hand signal. Did he hold it? If he did, go back to him and praise him. If he didn't, use the leash to correct him (snap and release) and try it again.

OFF-LEASH CONTROL

One of the biggest mistakes many dog owners make is to take their dog off the leash too soon. When you take your dog off the leash, you have very little control. If you take your dog off leash before you have established enough control or before your dog is mentally mature enough to accept that control, you are setting yourself up for disaster.

Poodles are smart, curious dogs and they love to check out new things, especially new smells. Rabbits, butterflies, and birds were made to chase, as far as Poodles are concerned. More than one Poodle has been so involved in his exploring that he's forgotten to pay attention to his owner's commands.

Before your Poodle is allowed off leash (outside of a fenced yard or your backyard), you need to make sure that his training is sound, which means he should be responding well to all of the basic commands.

Your Poodle must also be mentally mature. In some Poodles, that might be two, two-and-a-half, or even three years of age. (Toy Poodles are usually grown up by two years old, but many Standard Poodles are not mentally mature until three.) He should be past the challenging teenage stage of development. Never take a young adolescent off leash outside of a fenced-in area. That is setting the young dog up for a problem.

Come on a Long Line

The long line or leash was introduced earlier for teaching the come command. It is also a good training technique for preparing your dog for off-leash control. Review that section and practice the come command on the long line until you are comfortable that your dog understands how to come from 20 to 30 feet away.

Now take him out to play in a different but safe place, such as a schoolyard. Let your Poodle drag his long line behind him as you let him sniff and explore. When he's distracted and not paying attention to you, call him to come. If he responds right away, praise him enthusiastically and tell him what a smart wonderful dog he is.

If he doesn't respond right away, step on the end of the long line, pick it up, and back away from your dog, calling him again as you use the line to make him come to you. Don't beg him to come to you or repeat the come command. Simply use the line to make him do it. The come is not an optional command.

Heel

Most public places require your dog to have a leash; however, teaching your Poodle to heel without one is a good exercise. Not only is it a part of obedience competition (for people interested in that sport), but it's a good practical command, too. What would happen if your dog's leash or collar broke when you were out for a walk? Accidents happen and if your dog has already been trained to heel off leash, disaster would be averted.

To train your dog to heel, hook two leashes up to his collar. Use your regular leash and then a lightweight leash. Do a "watch me" exercise with treats and then tell your dog to heel. Practice walking slowly and quickly, turning corners, and performing figure eights. When your dog is paying close attention, reach down and

unhook his regular leash, tossing it to the ground in front of him. If he bounces up and assumes that he's free, correct him with the second leash, "Hey! I didn't release you!" and make him sit in the heel position. Hook his regular leash back up and repeat the exercise.

When he doesn't take advantage of the regular leash being taken off, tell him to heel and start practicing. Use the second leash for control and not for minor corrections. If he

If your Poodle likes to pull you along when he's on a leash, try a no-pull training halter that is guaranteed by the manufacturer to stop any dog of any size from ever pulling again. It's like having power steering for your dog. Photo courtesy of Four Paws.

tries to dash away, pull from you, or break the heel exercise, use that second leash and then hook his regular leash back on again.

Repeat this exercise, going back and forth between the two leashes, until he's not even thinking about whether his regular leash is on or not. You want him to work reliably without questioning the leash's control. For some Poodles, this may take several weeks of work.

When he is working reliably, put the second leash away. Take his regular leash and tuck it in his collar between his shoulder blades so that it is

Expect and demand the same level of obedience off leash that you do on leash, which includes heeling reliably. This Poodle demonstrates his perfect technique.

lying on his back. Practice his heel work. If he makes a mistake, grab the leash and collar as a handle and correct him. When the correction is over, take your hand off.

Expect and demand the same level of obedience off leash that you do on leash. Don't make excuses for off-leash work.

DOG SPORTS

Do you like training your Poodle? If so, you may want to try one or more dog activities or sports. Some are competitive, some are for fun, and others are for charity work. It's up to you to decide which activities work best for you and your Poodle.

Conformation Competition

The American Kennel Club (AKC) and the United Kennel Club (UKC) both award conformation championships to purebred dogs. The requirements vary between the registries, but a championship is awarded when a purebred dog competes against other dogs of his breed and wins. The judge compares each dog against a written standard for his breed and chooses the dog that most closely represents that standard

Photo by Isabelle Francais

Conformation competition might be a rewarding activity for you and your show-quality Poodle.

of excellence.

If you feel that your Poodle could compete in such a competition, go to some local dog shows. Watch the Poodles that are competing and talk to some of the owners and handlers. Does your Poodle still look like a good candidate? You will also want to read more about the breed and the conformation competition. It might even be beneficial to attend a conformation class.

Keep in mind that Poodles that are shown in conformation competition are groomed in a specific fashion. Can you keep your Poodle's coat in good condition? Keeping your poodle properly groomed for competition is a big commitment.

Obedience Competition

Obedience competition is a sport that you can do with your Poodle. Both of you are judged on your teamwork and ability to perform the set exercises in the course.

Both the AKC and the UKC sponsor obedience competitions for all breeds of dog, as do some other organizations, including the Poodle Club of America. There are also independent obedience competitions or tournaments held all over the country.

Before you begin training, write to the sponsoring organization and get a copy of the rules and regulations pertaining to competitions. Go to a few local dog shows and

In obedience competition, both the owner and the Poodle are judged on their teamwork and their ability to perform the set exercises in the course.

Photo by Isabelle Francais

watch the obedience competitions. See which dogs win and which don't. What did they each do differently? There are also a number of books available specifically addressing obedience competition. You may want to find a trainer in your area who specializes in competition training.

Canine Good Citizen

The Canine Good Citizen (CGC) program was instituted by the AKC in an effort to promote and reward responsible dog ownership. During a CGC test, the dog and owner must complete a series of ten exercises, including sitting for petting and

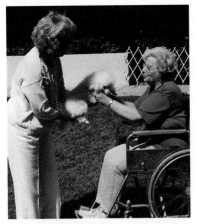

Poodles are affectionate and make terrific therapy dogs.

grooming, walking nicely on the leash, and performing the sit, down, stay, and come commands. Upon the successful completion of all ten exercises, the dog is awarded the CGC title.

For more information about CGC tests, contact a dog trainer or dog training club in your area.

Temperament Test

The American Temperament Test Society was founded to provide breeders and trainers with a means of uniformly evaluating a dog's temperament. By using standardized tests, each dog would be tested in the same manner. The tests can be used to evaluate potential breeding stock and future working dogs,

All Poodles need to be groomed. Your local pet shop sells excellent grooming supplies, which can sometimes be purchased in affordable combination packages. Photo courtesy of Wahl, USA.

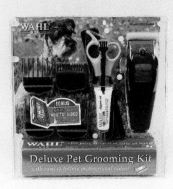

or simply as a way for dog owners to see how their dog might react in any given situation. For information about temperament tests in your area, contact a local trainer or dog training club.

Flyball

Flyball is a great sport for dogs that are crazy about tennis balls. Teams of four dogs and their owners compete against each other. Each dog runs down the course, jumps four hurdles, and then triggers the mechanism that spits out a tennis ball. The dog then catches the ball, turns, jumps the four hurdles again, and returns to his owners. The first team to complete the relay wins. Because Poodles are very athletic and quick, they do very well in this sport. If your Poodle likes to retrieve, this might be the activity for you.

Therapy Dogs

Dog owners have known for years that dogs are good company, but now researchers are agree that dogs are good medicine. Therapy dogs go to nursing homes, hospitals, and children's centers to provide warmth, affection, and love to the people who need it most. Poodles make great therapy

AGILITY

Agility is a fast-paced sport in which the dog must complete a series of obstacles in a certain period of time, with the fastest time winning. Obstacles might include tunnels, hurdles, an elevated dog walk, and more. The AKC, the UKC, and the United States Dog Agility Association all sponsor agility competitions. Because they are fast, agile, and intelligent, Poodles do very well in agility.

dogs! For more information, contact your local dog trainer about a group in your area.

You can make any Poodle look like a show champion. If you admire the fluffy, well-groomed look of show dogs, consider using a hair dryer on your dog after his bath. Start using it when he's a puppy so he will learn to enjoy the experience. Photo courtesy of Metropolitan Vacuum Cleaner Co., Inc.

Have Some
FUN
With Your Training!

Training can and should be fun. Although a lot of training consists of teaching your Poodle to control himself, it should also be enjoyable. Your Poodle is more apt to want to cooperate with your training if you can laugh together while you do it. Besides just simply having fun, games and trick training can challenge your training skills and your Poodle's ability to learn. In addition, you can have a great time showing off your very talented Poodle.

SHAKE HANDS

Shaking hands is a very easy trick to teach. Have your dog sit in front of you. Reach behind one front paw and as you say, "Shake!" tickle his leg in the hollow part just behind his paw. When he lifts his paw, shake it gently and praise him. When he starts lifting his paw on his own, stop tickling him.

WAVE

When your dog is shaking hands reliably, tell him "Shake. Wave!" and instead of shaking his paw, reach toward it without taking it. Let him touch

PLAY DEAD

I taught one of my dogs to play dead and we both had a lot of fun with it. Michi became so good that he could pick the phrase "dead dog" out of casual conversation. One day, Michi and I visited the son of a neighbor of mine who had just graduated from the police academy and was very proud of his new uniform. As I congratulated the new officer and shook his hand, I turned to Michi and asked, "Would you rather be a cop or a dead dog?" Michi dropped to the ground, went flat on his side, and closed his eyes. The only thing giving him away was the wagging tail. Meanwhile, my neighbor's son was stuttering and turning red. He didn't know whether to be offended or to laugh. It was great fun!

his paw to your hand, but pull your hand away so that he's waving. Praise him. Eventually you want him to lift his paw higher than for the shake and to move it up and down so he looks like he's waving. You can do that with the movements of your hand as he reaches for it. Praise him enthusiastically when he does it right. When he understands the wave, you can stop your hand movements.

ROLL OVER

With your Poodle lying down, take a treat and make a circle with your hand around his nose as you tell him, "Roll over." Use the treat (in a circular motion) to lead his head in the direction you want him to roll. Your other hand may have to help him. Standard Poodles have a big rib cage and it may take some effort on your dog's part to start the roll over movement.

WAIT FOR IT

Have your Poodle sit and stay. Set a treat on the top of his nose. Keep one hand under his chin to hold him steady as you tell him, "Wait for it!" After

Poodles have been used in circuses for several centuries because they learn tricks easily. They love to be the center of attention.

Photo by Isabelle Francais

a few seconds, take your hand away from his chin as you tell him, "Okay!" If he just drops the treat, let him go for it. If he catches it in mid-air, praise him enthusiastically. Some dogs learn how to flip the treat in the air and catch it before it hits the ground.

RETRIEVING

Most Poodles like to retrieve, they just don't always understand the need to bring back what they go out after. However, once you teach your Poodle to bring back the toy, retrieving games can be great fun, as well as good exercise.

If your Poodle likes to retrieve, then all you need to do is get him to bring the toy back to you. When you throw the toy and he goes after it, wait until he picks it up. Once he has it in his mouth, call him top lips against his teeth. You don't have to use much pressure, just enough so that he opens his mouth to relieve the pressure. When he gives you the toy, praise him.

If your Poodle likes to take the toy and run with it, let him drag his long line behind him while he plays. Then, when he dashes off, you can step on the line and stop him. Once you've stopped him, call him back to you.

THE NAME GAME

The name game is a great way to make your dog think. When you teach your Poodle the names of various objects around the house, you can then put him to work, too. Tell him to pick up your keys or your purse, or send him after the TV remote control.

Start with two items that are very different, perhaps a tennis ball and a magazine. Sit on the floor with your Poodle and place the two items in front of you. Ask him, "Where's the ball?" and bounce the ball so that he tries to grab it or at least pays attention to it. When he touches the ball, praise him and give him a treat.

When he is responding to the ball, lay it on the floor and send him after it. Praise and reward

---

MAKE UP YOUR OWN TRICKS

What would you and your Poodle have fun doing? Teach him to stand up on his back legs and dance. Teach him to jump through a hula hoop or your arms. Teach him to play dead or to sneeze. Only your imagination and your ability to teach your dog will limit trick training.

---

back to you in a happy tone of voice. If he drops the toy, send him back to it. If he brings the toy all the way back to you, praise him enthusiastically.

Don't let him play tug-of-war with the toy. If he grabs it and doesn't want to let go, reach over the top of his muzzle and tell him "Give," as you press his

Most Poodles like to retrieve, and if you teach your dog how to bring back the ball as well as fetch it, the two of you will have lots of fun.

Photo by Isabelle Francais

him. Now set several different items out with the magazine and ball and send him after the ball again. When he is doing well, start all over again with one of his toys. When he will get his toy, then put the toy and ball out there together and send him after one or the other. Don't correct him if he makes a mistake, just take the toy away from him and try it again. Remember that he's learning a foreign language, while at the same time trying to figure out what the game is, so be patient.

FIND IT!

When your Poodle can identify a few items by name, you can start hiding those things so that he can search for them. For example, once he

knows the word keys, you can drop your keys on the floor

The name game is a great way to make your dog think. Teach him the names of his toys or household objects, then amaze your friends with your Poodle's cleverness.

FIND THE CAR!

Take your Poodle out to your car and touch the side of the car as you tell him, "Find the car." When you touch the car, give him a treat. Do this several times a day for several days. Then have him touch the car (with his nose or a paw) before you give him the treat. Do this for several days. Then take him away from the car (down the block) and tell him, "Find the car!" Have him lead you to the car. Make him touch it before you give him the treat to eliminate any shortcuts. As he learns to do this, start making it more difficult. You'll be amazed how good he will be and you'll never lose your car again—at least not while your Poodle is with you!

Trick training is limited only by your imagination and your ability to teach your dog. What would you and your Poodle have fun doing?

Photo by Robert Pearcy

under an end table next to the sofa. Tell your Poodle, "Find my keys!" and help him look. "Where are they?" and move him toward the end table. When he finds them, praise him enthusiastically.

As he gets more adept, make the game more challenging by having him search in more than one room. Have the item hiding in plain sight or underneath something else. In the beginning, help him when he appears confused, but don't let him give up. Make sure that he succeeds.

HIDE AND SEEK

Start by having a family member pet your Poodle, offer him a treat, and go to another room. Tell your Poodle, "Find Dad!" and let him go. If he runs right to Dad, praise him. Have different family members play the game and teach the dog a name for each of them so that he can search for each family member by name.

As he gets better at the game, the family member hiding will no longer have to pet the dog at the beginning of the game—he can simply go hide. Help your dog so that he can succeed at the game, but also encourage him to use his nose and scenting abilities.

SUGGESTED READING

Books By T.F.H. Publications

JG 129
A New Owner's Guide to Poodles
Charlotte Schwartz
160 pages, 150 color photos

TS 283
Training Problem Dogs
Dr. Louis Vine
256 pages, 50 drawings

JG 109
Training the Perfect Puppy
Andrew DePrisco
160 pages, over 200 color photos

JG 117
*The New Owner's Guide
to Dog Training*
Dorman Pantfoeder
160 pages, over 100 full-color
photos